Symbols

🚗₁₀₀	Car parking (and number of spaces)
	No Parking
	Coach parking (may be by appointment only)
WC	Wc's
⛱	Picnic site
	Pub within 1 mile
🚲	Cycling
	Dogs allowed
	Dogs allowed on leads only
	Dogs not allowed
i	Information leaflet
i	Information board(s)
☞₁₂	Self-guided trail (and number of trails)
🚶(£)	Guided walks (£ = charge) (usually by appointment only)
👫	Schools welcome (usually by appointment only)
	Education materials

● ## Centre of Excellence

recognised by the Forestry Authority as demonstrating excellent standards in managing woodland for improving the quality of the landscape, creating benefits for wildlife, providing access for people, and growing timber in environmentally sound ways.

● ## Duke of Cornwall's Award:

for forestry and conservation. The premier award of the Royal Forestry Society.

C

We

Ho

Welcome!

Sunlight through the fresh green of young beech leaves; the smell of bracken under pillars of pine; a wash of bluebells through an oak wood; vivid red toadstools under autumn birches; a deer leaping across the track; the drumming of a distant woodpecker ....

A walk in the woods lifts the spirit as well as stretching the legs, and in such a crowded part of the world we are remarkably fortunate to have so many woods that welcome visitors. This book gives details of more than 120 of them. They vary in size from hundreds of hectares down to a few, and from sophisticated woodland parks with many visitor facilities to woods with no special provisions apart from a welcome for you to walk.

Some of the woods are publicly owned, others owned by charities such as the Woodland Trust, National Trust, and wildlife trusts, and some are privately owned. This is the only guidebook that gives details of a number of these woods.

Whilst the owners have different priorities for their woodlands, all are working towards some balance between wildlife and resource conservation, timber and wood production, and public access and recreation.

The county gazetteer sections are separated by articles about woodlands and trees in south east England and their history. They look at questions such as why there are so many woods in the Weald, and why the New Forest and Ashdown Forest are so lacking in trees.

At many of the places in this guide you have the opportunity to learn about and understand the wildlife and management of the wood, through trails, information panels and leaflets, and guided walks. The booklist at the back will help you to find out more.

We hope that using this guidebook will bring you much pleasure, and that it will remind you of woodlands that are old friends but perhaps you have not visited recently, as well as introducing you to new places.

Even better next time!

Do please help us to make the next edition even better by letting the Forestry Trust know of:

- Suggestions for woods that could be added to the guidebook

- Suggestions for improvements to the guidebook

- Any corrections or amendments needed.

Write to or telephone:

The Forestry Trust, The Old Estate Office, Englefield Road, Theale, Reading, Berks. RG7 5DZ. Tel: 0118 9323523 Fax: 0118 9304033

Collect other "Exploring Woodlands" guides

This is the first in a series of regional guidebooks that will eventually cover the whole of England and Wales. The next ones to be published will cover the West Country and the Severn and Wye valleys.

How to use this guidebook

★ The woods are arranged by county. Each county section has its own location map of woods.

★ The facilities at each wood are shown by symbols – see key inside front cover.

★ Where no car park is indicated, you may have to park on the roadside. Please take care not to cause an obstruction or damage.

★ School and group visits are welcome at many woods, but normally **by appointment only.**

★ A telephone number is given for each entry, for booking school and group visits, arranging guided walks, and obtaining information leaflets and educational materials where available.

★ Information on charges, opening arrangements and facilities is correct for 1998.

When you visit a wood, please

Respect the trees and wildlife, and take nothing away.

Keep the woodland free of litter and pollution.

Keep to paths, tracks and waymarked trails. Leave gates as you find them, open or shut.

If dogs are allowed, keep your dog under control.

Park your car where it will not cause obstruction. Take valuables with you if possible.

Be safety conscious, keeping clear of areas of forestry working.

Report anything untoward you may see on your walk.

Woodlands to visit in East Sussex

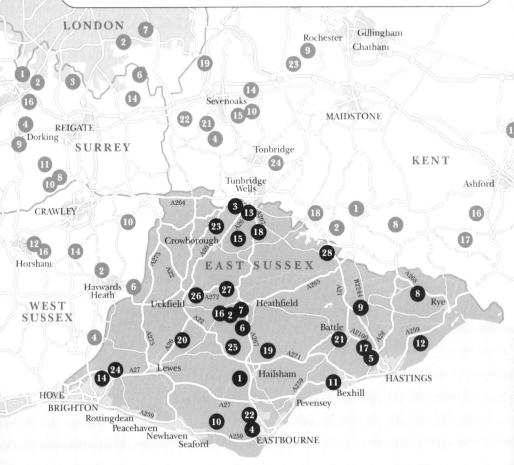

1	Abbotts Wood	10	Friston Forest	20	Plashett Wood
2	Blackdown Wood	11	Gillham Wood	21	Powdermill Wood
3	Broadwater Wood	12	Guestling Wood	22	Ratton Woodland
4	Cherry Garden Woods	13	Hargate Forest	23	Rocks Wood
5	Church-in-the-Wood	14	Hollingbury Woods	24	Stanmer Great Wood
6	Coney Burrow	15	Hornshurst Wood	25	Twenty Acre Wood
7	Darch's Wood	16	Kiln Wood	26	Views Wood
8	Flatropers Wood	17	Marline Wood	27	Wilderness Wood
9	Footland Wood	18	Nap Wood	28	Yellowcoat Wood
		19	Park Wood		

0 5 10 15 20 25 30 Kms
0 5 10 15 20 Miles
N

© Arka Cartographics Ltd. 1998

1. ABBOTS WOOD
ARLINGTON
Tel: (01580) 211044
TQ556074

(Forest Enterprise) 356 ha. (880 acres)

Take the A22 S from the Boship roundabout. Turn R on to minor road after approximately 2 miles, then take the next L. The car park is on the L 400 yds. beyond The Old Oak public house.

Part of the old Wilmington Forest, this wood has a long history of continuous management. There are mature hardwood and conifers as well as more recently planted areas. The lake is a central point of interest and the wood is well known for its flora, especially during the spring. BBQ's for hire. Education service.

Open: Free access at all times. Extensive rides and paths with waymarked routes. Wheelchair path.

---

2. BLACKDOWN WOOD
BLACKBOYS
Tel: (01825) 733211
TQ538202

(D. E. Gunner) 3 ha. (7 ½ acres)

Take the B2102 E from Blackboys village. In ¼ mile turn R to Waldron. Lay-by is ¾ mile on R side of road after bridge.

Bus 141 along B2102.

Rotational cutting of chestnut coppice with oak and Scots pine standards. 12 year old amenity planting of indigenous species. Excellent display of bluebells in May. Attractive walk by the stream.

Open: 08.00 to sunset, all year. Public footpath along stream. Permissive bridleway. Open access to adjoining fields managed under Countryside Stewardship Scheme.

---

3. BROADWATER WOOD
GROOMBRIDGE
Tel: (01323) 811329
TQ555373

(Privately owned; managed by Fountain Forestry) 55.4 ha. (137 acres)

Take the A26 S from Tunbridge Wells. 1 mile after leaving the edge of town turn R at crossroads. Follow road for 1 mile, car park will be on R.

Situated on level ground approximately ½ mile from High Rocks, surrounded by woodland and farmland. Production of softwood timber is a primary objective. Maturing stands of Scots pine, together with areas of mixed broadleaf and open heath. Sandy soils mean good underfoot conditions for most of the year. New car park and extensive trail building planned for 1998. Very popular with dog walkers. Orienteering organised by local group several times a year.

Open: Free access at all times. Extensive rides and paths, no public rights of way.

---

4. CHERRY GARDEN WOODS
EASTBOURNE
Tel: (01323) 415279
TV588990

(Eastbourne Borough Council) 14 ha. (36 acres)

Take the A259 from Eastbourne towards Seaford. Car park adjacent to Youth Hostel, on N side of road on the edge of Eastbourne.

Buses 711 and 712 stop 20m. from Youth Hostel.

A narrow strip of woodland on the scarp slope of the South Downs, between an urban area and downland golf course. Ride management and thinning/removal works carried out along main access routes. Groups of elm throughout woodland of ash and sycamore, with some beech. Areas of planting and natural regeneration from the 1987 storm have recently been thinned and protective spirals removed.

Open: Free access at all times. Jubilee Way runs through central wooded area, and access along rides.

---

5.   **CHURCH-IN-THE-WOOD**
      HASTINGS
      Tel: (01424) 722022
      TQ

(Hastings Borough Council)
25 ha. (62 acres)

Head S for approx. 2½ miles from junction of the A2100 and B2092 (Queensway). Turn L into Churchwood Drive, follow the road for ¾ mile before turning R into Church-in-the-Wood Lane. Follow road past church into car park.

Church-in-the-Wood is an ancient woodland site formerly managed under a coppice system and dominated by oak, sweet chestnut and hornbeam. Severely damaged by the 1987 hurricane, but coppicing has since been reintroduced under the Forestry Commission's Woodland Grant Scheme.

Open: Free access at all times. Extensive rides and paths.

---

6.   **CONEY BURROW**
      HORAM
      Tel: (01435) 812597
      TQ577175

(Major M.R.R. Goulden)
20 ha. (49 acres)

On A267 between Heathfield and Hailsham on S side of Horam village; on W side of road.

Woods, streams and lakes.   Part new conifers, part ancient hornbeam woods with open fields, which give the nature walks a unique and varied interest at all times of the year. Totally unspoilt by exploitation, this is one of the most beautiful parts of the Sussex Low Weald - home of the old Sussex iron industry. Refreshments. Children's farm. Craft workers.

Open: 10.00 - 17.00 every day, Easter to October. Winter months by appointment. Marked paths.

Charges: Voluntary contribution 50p.

---

7.   **DARCH'S WOOD**
      CROSS-IN-HAND
      Tel: (01435) 862351
      TQ569215

(Cross-in-Hand Amenities Society)
16 ha. (40 acres)

At Cross-in-Hand turn S into A267 Eastbourne Road.   Shortly on R is St. Bartholomews Church and car park. Entrance to wood is behind church.

The managed woodland has many mature trees, but extensive replanting took place after the storm of 1987. Over the coming period the area around the new saplings will be cleared to allow an open canopy for their growth. The woodland enjoys a network of small paths and a lake, and contains many wild flowers and birds.

Open: Free access at all times. Extensive network of paths for walking.

---

8. FLATROPERS WOOD
RYE
Tel: (01273) 492630
TQ861231

(Sussex Wildlife Trust)
35 ha. (86 acres)

Entrance is on Bixley Lane, which leaves the A268 on the S side of a sharp bend S of Beckley.

A beautiful example of typical E. Sussex woodland. In many parts young birch has been cut and regenerates profusely on the sandy soils of this area. Sweet chestnut has been cut as coppice, and there are small plantations of beech and pine. Standard oaks provide a continuity of woodland cover and more are being planted into the area of cut birch - the birch being a timber crop. An open heathy ride crosses the reserve and the sunny woodland tracks and paths support many invertebrates such as the pearl bordered fritillary and the tiger beetle. The spread of heather is encouraged by controlling bracken and birch.

Open: Free access at all times. There is good access throughout along a system of paths and rides.

9. FOOTLAND WOOD
WHATLINGTON
Tel: (01528) 211044
TQ764204

(Forest Enterprise) 167 ha. (412 acres)

From the A21 S of John's Cross take the B2089 eastwards. The car park is on the R some 600 yards distant.

A mixed conifer/broadleaf woodland with a variety of tree species and ages. Although it suffered greatly in the storm of 1987, there are still areas of mature conifers to be seen within the valley bottoms and in the adjacent Barnes Wood.

Open: Free access at all times. Extensive ride and path network.

10. FRISTON FOREST
FRISTON
Tel: (01528) 211044
TQ519001

(Forest Enterprise) 858 ha. (2,119 acres)

Take the A259 W from Eastbourne. At the Seven Sisters Country Park at Exceat, take the minor road to Litlington on the R. The car park is on the R, 100 yards beyond the R turn to West Dean village.

Bus 711 and 712. along A259 to Seven Sisters Country Park.

The woodlands are predominantly beech and were planted mostly between the two world wars. There are waymarked walks from both car parks which are situated on opposite sides of the forest and the extensive network enables the more adventurous walker to venture further afield. There are several sites of botanical interest where typical chalk downland plant communities may be found and there is a National Nature Reserve managed by English Nature on the northern edge of the forest. BBQ's for hire. Education service.

Open: Free access at all times. Extensive rides and paths, plus waymarked routes.

11. GILLHAM WOOD
BEXHILL
Tel: (01273) 492630
TQ718069

(Sussex Wildlife Trust) 3.2ha. (8 acres)

Off Gillham Wood Road in Bexhill. Access to the woodland is from the lay-by on the N side of Withyham Road, Cooden.

This oak woodland, within a residential area, has altered little over the years. Beneath the trees is a thick shrub layer with bramble beneath. Most of the oak is of similar age and size, indicating that the wood was probably felled about 50 years ago and allowed to redevelop naturally.
Management is centred around maintaining the footpath network and opening glades to encourage butterflies and woodland flowers.

Open: Free access at all times.

---

12.   GUESTLING WOOD
HASTINGS
Tel: (01476) 581111
TQ863148

(Woodland Trust) 22ha. (53 acres)

From Hastings take the A259 to Rye. On the outskirts of Hastings turn R towards Pett. In Pett village at a sign for a caravan park turn L along Watermill Lane and continue to the Woodland Trust's car park on the L.

Bus (Hastings to Rye) stops at Guestling Green, from where numerous public footpaths run to Guestling Wood.

An area of ancient woodland, dominated by sweet chestnut coppice with oak standards. Where the wood slopes towards the stream on its western edge the chestnut gives way to hazel, birch, willow and alder. In spring the woodland floor is covered by wood anemones and bluebells.

Open: Free access at all times. Good network of footpaths and rides. Dogs must be on leads at all times because there are usually sheep on surrounding farmland.

13.   HARGATE FOREST
TUNBRIDGE WELLS
Tel: (01476) 581111
TQ575369

(Woodland Trust) 60ha. (148 acres)

Take the A267 S from Tunbridge Wells. Take first road R beyond edge of town (c. ½ mile). Entrance is about ½ mile on L.

A mixed conifer/broadleaf woodland providing an enjoyable circular walk. The woodland will be managed as mixed high forest, using natural regeneration of both conifers and broadleaves. Ongoing thinning will permit the better quality trees more room to grow and, allied to control of the dense rhododendrons, will permit natural regeneration to flourish. An excellent site for butterflies.

Open: Free access at all times. Extensive rides marked on information board at main entrance.

---

14.   HOLLINGBURY WOODS
BRIGHTON
Tel: (01273) 292140
TQ315078

(Brighton & Hove Council)
5 ha. (12.5 acres)

Take the Ditchling Road out of Brighton to the entrance to Hollingbury Golf Club opposite Woodborne Garage.

The wood was badly damaged by the storm in 1987, following which The Friends of Hollingbury and Burstead Woods was set up to manage its recovery. They have carried out a lot of tree planting and after care, as well as installing a nature trail and maintaining glade areas. Children's playground adjacent.

Open: Free access at all times. Public open

space with footpaths.

15. HORNSHURST WOOD
ROTHERFIELD
Tel: (01323) 811329
TQ556309

(Privately owned; managed by Fountain Forestry) 57 ha. (141 acres)

Take B2100 into Rotherfield. In village centre take minor road N towards Eridge. Car park is ³/₄ mile on L, about 100 yds. after cemetery.

Situated in the heart of the High Weald AONB and surrounded by woodland and farmland, the wood is atop a ridge and slopes down to a bubbling stream to the west. Good views from many points. Production of softwood timber is a primary objective, with semi-mature stands of Corsican pine, together with areas replanted after the 1987 storm. Sandy soils mean good underfoot conditions for most of the year. Stream side walks are being created in 1998, together with benches and information boards. Horse riding run by the Rotherfield Woodland Riding Club. Very popular with dog walkers and increasingly with cyclists. Orienteering by arrangement with Bowles Outdoor Centre.

Open: Free access at all times. Extensive rides and paths, and two rights of way.

16. KILN WOOD
BLACKBOYS
Tel: (01476) 581111
TQ527203

(Woodland Trust) 8 ha. (20 acres)

Take the B2102 from Uckfield to Heathfield. Turn R on to B2192 at Blackboys and after ¹/₂ mile turn L down Hollow Lane. Park in lay by on L at bottom of hill.

A mixture of mature and recently planted woodland, all accessible via a circular route. Bluebells abound in the western section of the wood where wild service and midland hawthorn can also be found.

Open: Free access at all times. Extensive network of rides.

17. MARLINE WOOD
HASTINGS
Tel: (01273) 492630
TQ783123

(Sussex Wildlife Trust) 40 ha. (99 acres)

Off the Queensway NW of Hastings. Park in Napier Road and enter by public footpath.

Much of Marline Wood is old hornbeam coppice, now being restored. Part of the wood is a ghyll, a steep sandstone valley with bare rock faces. Here the moist, sheltered microclimate allows a variety of rare mosses and liverworts to flourish. The Marline Valley reserve as a whole includes flower rich meadows and some areas of scrub heavily used by migrant birds.

Open: Free access at all times. Keep out of the ghyll (river gorge) – it is dangerous and contains many rare mosses and liverworts.

18. NAP WOOD
FRANT
Tel: (01892) 890651
TQ583327

(The National Trust) 45 ha. (111 acres)

Take the A267 S from Tunbridge Wells. Nap Wood is about 2 miles S of Frant, on the L opposite a minor turning to the R. Park on the verge.

Bus 252 along A267.

Ancient woodland with sandstone stream valleys. A Sussex Wildlife Trust reserve. The oak, whilst the dominant tree in the wood, gives way to areas of chestnut coppice and clumps of pine planted in certain areas. In many parts of the reserve the oaks have grown up as wide spreading standard trees, but near the entrance they have been cut and worked as coppice. Streams have cut steep valleys forming moist habitats for mosses, liverworts and ferns more commonly found in the N and W of Britain. Controlling bracken and rhododendron helps to preserve the oldest beeches which are attractive for both wildlife and visitors.

Open: Free access at all times. One circular walk.

---

19. PARK WOOD
HELLINGLY
Tel: (01273) 482670
TQ603125

(Environment Agency)   60 ha. (148 acres)

From the A271, travelling E from Upper Horsebridge, turn L on to the minor road C208 (signed Hellingly Hosp.). Approx. 1½ miles on towards Grove Hill (about ½ mile from Hellingly Hospital) the car park is indicated on the R by a fingerpost.

An ancient semi-natural lowland woodland designated as a Site of Nature Conservation Interest. It is principally a deciduous oak woodland with a long history of coppice management which is still being carried out. Significant areas of coppice hornbeam, hazel and sweet chestnut can be found here, together with the second oldest cherry in the county and a 200 year old beech tree. The wood slopes gently to the SW and boasts streams, a pond and wetland area, old boundary banks, relics of the Wealden iron industry and remnants of camps built by the Canadians during the second world war.

Badgers, deer and rabbits can be seen in the wood. Interpretation boards are planned for installation in summer 1998 covering management of the wood, its history, and coppicing.

Open: Free access at all times. Extensive rides and paths, experimental bridleway, surfaced path, disabled trail. Three waymarked routes.

---

20. PLASHETT WOOD
LEWES/UCKFIELD
Tel: (01273) 401590

(I. V. Askew Charitable Trust)
150 ha. (371 acres)

The wood is alongside the A26, halfway between Lewes and Uckfield.

Buses 728, 141 along A26.

A predominantly oak ancient broadleaved woodland, managed for timber production, nature conservation and shooting. An educational programme is being developed. Plashett Wood is the largest block of broadleaved woodland under one management plan in East Sussex. The wood is managed as a working woodland and has a resident charcoal producer as well as various other value-adding activities.

Open: Access by appointment only and with the forester as a guide (£). Extensive rides and paths.

---

21. POWDERMILL WOOD
BATTLE
Tel: (01424) 773817
TQ735143

(R. Cope)   38 ha. (93 acres)

On B2095 between Battle and Catsfield. Car park is on N side of road, ½ mile from western

end of road.

This ancient woodland has a very varied topography with a wide range of tree species. It is managed for timber production as well as conservation. Much of the wood is rotationally coppiced (mainly sweet chestnut). There are two nature reserves covering the wettest areas, one managed by Sussex Wildlife Trust, the other by the Powdermill Trust. Guided walks and woodcraft courses can be organised by arrangement. Wood products for sale.

Open: Free access at all times. Waymarked trail. Two public rights of way.

---

22. RATTON WOODLAND
WILLINGDON
Tel: (01323) 415279
TQ579017

(Eastbourne Borough Council)
22 ha. (54 acres)

From the main roundabout in Willingdon on the A22, take turning to Willingdon village. Follow Butts Lane to car park.

Buses 126 and 218 to village post office. (Buses 214/215 Sunday)

Growing on steep downland scarp slopes above the town, the woodland has a wide variety of tree species and age classes. There are newly planted areas mixed with regeneration following the 1987 storm, and pole stage ash and sycamore. There is a dense area of yews, mature beech, lime and horse chestnut, and small clumps of pine and holm oak. Coppicing is carried out at ride sides to let in light, with thinning works throughout the area.

Open: Free access at all times. Extensive network of footpaths, bridleways and timber extraction rides.

23. ROCKS WOOD
GROOMBRIDGE
Tel: (01892) 867434
TQ525350

(Lord and Lady Gibson) 17ha. (42 acres)

From the B2110 between Groombridge and Crowborough, take minor road E signed Motts Mill. Through Motts Mill at the top of a very steep hill turn R.

Approximately 17 ha. of predominantly sweet chestnut coppice with three small areas of coniferous woodland. Three pleasant walks available with glimpses of interesting rock formations. Archaeological excavations in 1982 produced mesolithic "finds", pottery of several periods and also a bowl furnace for iron working. Fallow deer, badgers, foxes and rabbits may be seen and a good variety of birds, flowers and plants are present all year round.

Open: Free access all year, 09.00 – 16.00, along rides. Please respect privacy of local residents.

---

24. STANMER GREAT WOOD
BRIGHTON
Tel: (01273) 292140
TQ343087

(Brighton & Hove Council)
60 ha. (150 acres)

From the A27 E of Brighton, follow signs for Stanmer Park. The Great Wood is on the L of the park before the house.

Various buses to park entrance on A27 (for Sussex University). Nearest station is Falmer.

Stanmer Great Wood is part of Stanmer Park, 440 ha. of mixed woodland, farmland and park land just outside Brighton which was acquired by the council in 1949. Great Wood was extensively planted in the 18th century to provide pleasant woodland walks (with the accompaniment of hidden musicians!) for the residents of Stanmer House. Some parts of the wood were severely damaged by the great storm in 1987 and much replanting has been undertaken since. Great Wood contains areas of mixed hazel and sweet chestnut coppice, which are the focus of a restoration programme now into its fifth year and are the best places to see woodland plants such as bluebells and yellow pimpernel. There is an annual open day in the spring when coppice crafts, heavy horses, etc., can be seen in the woods.

Open: Free access at all times. Extensive network of footpaths.

---

25. TWENTY ACRE WOOD
CHIDDINGLY
Tel: (01825) 872691
TQ539127

(A. Penrose) 8 ha. (20 acres)

Duke of Cornwall's Award

At Golden Cross on the A22, 11 miles N of Eastbourne, turn east for Chiddingly. The wood is 350m. on the right hand side, across a small field.

A 20 acre typical Sussex commercial wood, with coppice compartments originally designed to meet the needs of local farmers and builders. There are some good stands of oak, hornbeam, chestnut and hazel, all of which are being worked on rotation. The 1987 storm extensively damaged the wood and disrupted the coppice programme, but order is gradually returning. There is a good variety of herb plants, insects and birds, including several families of pied woodpeckers in the alder coppice by the stream.

Open: Dawn to dusk, all year. Rides and paths.

---

26. VIEWS WOOD
UCKFIELD
Tel: (01476) 581111
TQ479225

(Woodland Trust) 26 ha. (64 acres)

From Uckfield, take A26 N towards Heron's Ghyll. Before 40mph sign, turn R into Browns Lane, leading into Manor Park Estate. Park within housing estate, but please have due respect for residents.

Ancient semi-natural woodland, adjacent to Buxted Park. Sweet chestnut coppice dominates the site and bluebell, primrose, violet and wild daffodil bloom in the spring. Coppicing has been reintroduced into parts of the wood, whilst the rest will be managed as high forest.

Open: Free access at all times. Good network of rides.

---

27. WILDERNESS WOOD
HADLOW DOWN
Tel: (01825) 830509
TQ536240

(Chris and Anne Yarrow) 24 ha. (60 acres)

Duke of Cornwall's Award

Centre of Excellence

On S side of A272 in Hadlow Down village, 5 miles NE of Uckfield.

Buxted Station 3 miles; Bus 252 1 mile.

A very interesting working woodland managed by resident owner-occupier, a professional forester; to maximise timber, wildlife, education and recreation benefits. Mainly chestnut coppice cut on a 15 year cycle, with mixed age plantations of beech and conifers, and Christmas tree plantation. The produce is manufactured on site into garden furniture and products. Set in rolling High Weald AONB, with lovely views; springtime bluebells, autumn toadstools. An ancient woodland, with Roman iron smelting sites. Woodland trails and exhibition in timber barn give an insight into growing and using wood, and woodland wildlife. Adventure playground. Refreshments. Events programme. Guided walks, children's activities and "hands-on" demonstrations available for booked groups and schools.

Open: All year 10.00 - dusk. Extensive paths and rides. "Easy access" path.

Charges: Adults £1.90; OAPs/disabled £1.50; children £1.10.

Reduced rates Nov-Feb. 10% discount for booked groups.

Enterprise Centre being developed at Flimwell, comprising a visitor centre, exhibitions, shop and workshops specialising in wood manufacturing. As well as catering for children, schools and colleges, the demonstrations will also provide an enjoyable insight into the local "wood story" and stimulate interest in the sustainable development of our local woodland resources.

Open: Trails open to public in 1999, telephone for information on guided walks and events before then. Waymarked routes under development.

No charges for 1998. Entrance to visitor centre will be chargeable in 1999.

---

28. YELLOWCOAT WOOD
FLIMWELL
Tel: (01580) 879552
TQ715311

(East Sussex County Council - managed by Woodland Enterprises Ltd.)

23 ha. (57 acres)

Signposted from the A21, the entrance will be S of Flimwell crossroads with A268/B2087.

Bus to Flimwell crossroads.

This example of a working woodland shows examples of a range of High Weald woodland types. As well as mature and young conifer stands, examples of several stages of chestnut coppice growth can be seen. The woodland trail is being established as part of the Woodland

The most wooded part of England -why?

If you stand on the South Downs and look out over the hills of the Weald, the sea of wooded ridges could be the Saxon forest of Andredsweald. The Weald of Sussex, Surrey and west Kent is one of the most wooded parts of England. Some parishes have over 30% of their area under woodland, compared with 8% for England as a whole. Why is this?

Before our forefathers began the lengthy process of clearing the "wildwood", almost the whole country was blanketed in trees. By the time the Romans arrived, their predecessors had cleared perhaps half of the forest, and the Downs of

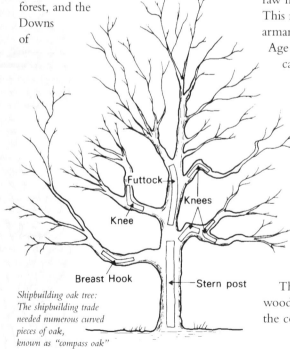

Shipbuilding oak tree:
The shipbuilding trade
needed numerous curved
pieces of oak,
known as "compass oak"

Sussex and Hampshire were probably as bare as they are today. The process of deforestation continued right up to the early twentieth century, by which time England had less forest than any European country - just 4%.

Charcoal for furnaces and forges

All along, the Weald was an exception. Partly this was because of its difficulties for farming - hilly landscape, infertile and badly drained soils, bad roads. But chiefly it was because its woods were too valuable to clear for farming. The charcoal that they provided was an essential industrial raw material for the Wealden iron industry. This nationally important industry supplied armaments from the spearheads of the Iron Age and Romans right through to the cannons of Tudor times. Charcoal also fuelled the gunpowder industry near Battle in Sussex, the Kent and Sussex hop-drying industries, glassworks in West Sussex and many local brickworks. The itinerant charcoal burners still found in a few woods in the late 1940's were the last vestige of a trade stretching back for 2,500 years.

"Wooden walls" from Wealden woods

The charcoal burners coppiced the woods on a cycle of 15 years or so. Above the coppice grew oak "standards", and these were the raw material for shipbuilding in timber. The shipyards and naval dockyards on the Thames and Solent needed a prodigious quantity of timber – about 2,000 mature oak trees for a single 74-gun eighteenth century warship.

Changing markets, neglected woods

The invention of iron ships ended the market for ships' timber; then in our own century, all available timber was felled during the two world wars. Wood and charcoal have been replaced by coke, oil and electricity as industrial raw materials and fuels. We are left with a beautiful landscape whose woods were once an essential part of the national and local economy, but are now historic relics. The reasons for the Wealden woods have gone – shipbuilding, iron smelting, hop-drying, gunpowder, glass – forgotten apart from a footnote to local history. The woods themselves are probably less tended than at any time in the last 1,000 years.

An uncertain future

Wealden woods are highly artificial, very different from the original "wildwood". What of their future? In one of the most densely peopled parts of the world, they are valued as places of beauty, peace and quiet, and havens for wildlife. Some are managed with these objectives paramount, particularly by bodies such as the Woodland Trust and county wildlife trusts, and by some private owners; but most are no longer managed at all.

Woodland is a uniquely adaptable multi-purpose resource, that can produce sustainable raw materials (wood and timber) as well as providing for recreation and enjoyment and conserving wildlife and landscape. In a country that imports 87% of its timber requirements, will we again adapt our Wealden woods to have a productive economic function, growing raw materials for wood-using industries and crafts?

Charcoal-burning in the seventeenth century

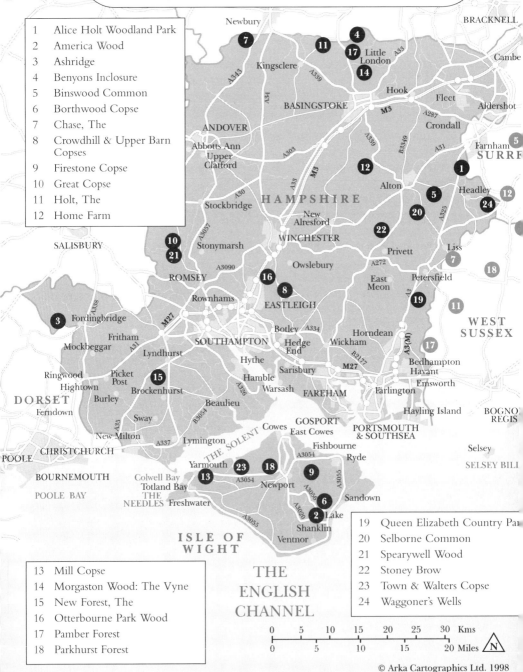

Woodlands to visit in Hampshire & Isle of Wight

1 Alice Holt Woodland Park
2 America Wood
3 Ashridge
4 Benyons Inclosure
5 Binswood Common
6 Borthwood Copse
7 Chase, The
8 Crowdhill & Upper Barn Copses
9 Firestone Copse
10 Great Copse
11 Holt, The
12 Home Farm

13 Mill Copse
14 Morgaston Wood: The Vyne
15 New Forest, The
16 Otterbourne Park Wood
17 Pamber Forest
18 Parkhurst Forest

19 Queen Elizabeth Country Park
20 Selborne Common
21 Spearywell Wood
22 Stoney Brow
23 Town & Walters Copse
24 Waggoner's Wells

THE ENGLISH CHANNEL

ISLE OF WIGHT

| 0 | 5 | 10 | 15 | 20 | 25 | 30 Kms |
| 0 | | 5 | 10 | | 15 | 20 Miles |

© Arka Cartographics Ltd. 1998

1. ALICE HOLT WOODLAND PARK
FARNHAM
Tel: (01420) 23666
SU88415

(Forest Enterprise) 925 ha. (2260 acres)

Follow the A325 S from Farnham for 4 miles. Turn L at crossroads by the Halfway House (PH). Car park is 400m. on the L.

Buses 18 and 38 Aldershot-Farnham; nearest stop Bucks Horn Oak.

Historic woodland managed for timber, visitors and wildlife. Varied woodlands with a mixture of broadleaved and coniferous trees of all ages. Plenty of wildlife, including purple emperor butterflies along the attractive rides, and stunning summer dragonflies by the lake and several ponds. Lots of birdlife - hear the hammering woodpeckers. Some ancient oaks remain, a reminder of the great oaks felled in the 17th century to build ships and construct the roof of the Great Hall of Westminster. Many waymarked trails to lead you safely through the peaceful forest. Visitor centre open weekends and school holidays, with refreshments; unusual souvenirs, and forest products. Attractive "play wood" play area. Day fishing permits. Education officer.

Open: 08.00 - 17.00 winter; 08.00 - 21.00 summer. Three waymarked routes, easy access trail, family cycle trail. Several public rights of way and bridleways.

Car parking charge: 50p for 1 hour; £1 all day, weekdays, £1.50 Sundays/ Bank Holidays.

2. AMERICA WOOD
SHANKLIN
Tel: (01476) 581111
SZ568819

(Woodland Trust) 11 ha. (27 acres)

1½ miles W of Shanklin between the A3056 and A3020. Park in nearby Shanklin or on one of the surrounding roads and walk to the wood.

Buses on the A3056 and A3020. Within walking distance from Shanklin Station.

America Wood is one of a few remnants of the deciduous woodland which once covered most of the Isle of Wight. It is a SSSI and a fine example of oak and birch ancient woodland. One story tells that the wood took on the name of America Wood after the American War of Independence in 1775, when most of the mature oak trees were felled for timber to build the naval ships which sailed from Britain to fight the war. During the storms of 1987 and 1990 parts of the wood were damaged and open areas were created. The oak and birch trees which dominate the wood form an interesting and unusual woodland type on strongly acid soils. The principal aim of management is to perpetuate the character of the oak woodland. Bats inhabit some of the old hollow treees and you may see red squirrels in the trees. Hemlock water dropwort grows profusely in the damper areas of the wood. It is one of Britain's most poisonous plants.

Open: Free access at all times. Extensive paths, including public footpaths and bridleways.

3. ASHRIDGE
SALISBURY
Tel: (01725) 518200
SU098153

(David J Dampney) 30 ha. (74 acres)

Take B3078 from Fordingbridge to Cranborne. Immediately W of Damerham turn L; after °mile turn R at signpost by telephone kiosk.

You may walk through an arboretum to open country with a 5 year old forestry spinney, leading on to 30 acres of semi-ancient woodland. This is high forest of oak and ash with hazel coppice, some of which is still in rotation. There are ponds and clearings, and a very varied flora including green hellebores, helleborines, orchids and bluebells.

Open: 9 April-2 July, Sundays and Bank Holidays; also National Gardens Scheme.

Charges: Adult £1.80; OAP £1.50; child 50p.

---

4. BENYON'S INCLOSURE
MORTIMER WEST END
SILCHESTER
Tel: 0118-930-2504
SU625640

(R.H.R. Benyon) 180 ha. (445 acres)

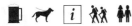

The wood is on the S side of the road from Mortimer going W towards Heath End, immediately after Mortimer West End. Roadside parking.

A coniferous forest, principally of Scots pine with Douglas fir and scattered broadleaved species. There is mainly alder in the valleys. Part of the wood is a County Heritage site.

Open: Free access at all times. Extensive rides and paths.

---

5. BINSWOOD COMMON
OAKHANGER & EAST
WORLDHAM
Tel: (01476) 581111
SU764370

(Woodland Trust) 62 ha. (153 acres)

S of the A31 and W of the A3.

Situated to the S of the B3004 (Green Street), a minor road from Alton to East Worldham. From the A31, via Alton to the B3004, go down the hill from East Worldham and turn R onto a road/track signposted as a bridleway. Park in Oakhanger or East Worldham and take one of the public footpaths which lead directly to the common.

Bus along B3004 to the N of the wood (Alton to Steaford). 3 miles from Alton Station.

Binswood is a woodland pasture common which has been designated as a SSSI and a County Heritage Site. It was once part of Woolmer Forest and used by King John for deer hunting. Henry IV reopened it in the 14th century for use by commoners. Binswood is now actively grazed by commoners and pollarding and coppicing has been reintroduced since the Woodland Trust acquired the site in 1985.

Open: Free access at all times, throughout the site.

---

6. BORTHWOOD COPSE
APSE HEATH, NR. SANDOWN
Tel: (01983) 740956
SZ567843

(National Trust) 24 ha. (60 acres)

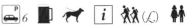

Take the A3056 from Newport to Sandown. Turn L at Apse Heath mini roundabout and the entrance is ½ mile on R (Alverstone Road).

Bus 91 to Winford, on Alverstone Road.

Borthwood is a fragment of a medieval hunting forest that covered much of the East Wight. It offers much variety, ranging from recently coppiced hazel, chestnut and oak glades to ancient oak trees and more recent Scots pine. It is a splendid place for carpets of bluebells in spring and autumn colour in October. Red squirrels, dormice, wood crickets and white admirals are some of its specialities.

Open: Free access during daylight hours all year. Extensive network of paths; bridleway and public footpath.

---

7. THE CHASE
BROADLAYINGS,
WOOLTON HILL
Tel: (01256) 881337
SU442630

(National Trust)   56 ha.   (138 acres)

3 miles SW of Newbury on the A343. Through Broadlayings, pass "Rampant Cat" public house. Car parking on Station Road.

Mixed conifer and broadleaved woodland. Conifer plantations not being replaced, but favour broadleaf replacements. Areas of natural regeneration of both conifer and broadleaves. Alder coppicing cycle along stream. Good show of snowdrops along stream in February.

Open: Free access from dawn to dusk daily. Extensive ride and path network.

---

8. CROWDHILL AND UPPER BARN COPSES
BISHOPSTOKE
Tel: (01476) 581111
SU485201

(Woodland Trust)   31 ha.   (77 acres)

Turn off the M3 at junction 10 on to the A33 S, then join the B3335. After 2 miles turn L towards Fisher's Pond. Crowdhill and Upper Barn Copses are set back from the road on the R just after Crowdhill. Enter the E edges of both copses from Crowdhill. Parking is available on Harding's Lane about ½ mile from the wood.

Buses run from Southampton through Crowdhill. Nearest station Southampton.

Both Crowdhill and Upper Barn Copses are thought to be ancient woodland sites and were once part of the Bishop of Winchester's hunting park. Both copses were planted with conifers during the 1950s and 1960s and so had lost much of their native broadleaved character until the Woodland Trust carried out a thinning operation in 1997/8. Upper Barn Copse is a mixed woodland consisting mainly of conifers, including Western hemlock, Norway spruce and Douglas fir. Beech, oak, ash, willow, silver birch and poplar are also present. The woodland ground flora includes yellow pimpernel, foxglove, wild angelica, wood violet and wood spurge as well as a profusion of bluebells. Crowdhill Copse is a similar but smaller copse and contains a greater density of oak trees. There is a steep-sided stream running through it which provides damp shady habitats for liverworts and mosses. Both copses support large populations of roe deer.

Open: Free access at all times. Pedestrian access around extensive rides.

---

9. FIRESTONE COPSE
WOOTTON
Tel: (01983) 522583
SZ559910

(Forest Enterprise)   98 ha.   (242 acres)

Just E of Wootton bridge, turn SE from the A3054. Follow the Firestone Copse road for 1 mile.

This attractive area of forest is notable for its delightful walks along grassy rides amidst pines, oaks and majestic spires of redwoods and grand fir. The grassy rides are full of wild flowers in spring, and in summer are home to a wide range of butterfly species. A sheltered trail and viewing screen in the trees gives bird watchers the opportunity to view the tidal Wootton Creek. Nationally important wood for red squirrel conservation.

Open: Free access at all times. Forest roads and rides. Two waymarked trails.

---

10. GREAT COPSE
MOTTISFONT, NR. ROMSEY
Tel: (01794) 340757
SU320282

(National Trust)   21 ha. (53 acres)

On the B3084 approx. 4 miles N of Romsey. R turning just N of Spearywell Wood. Or N from Mottisfont village, turning L after main entrance to Abbey.

Nearest station - Dunbridge.

An ancient, semi-natural wood with oak and ash over hazel coppice. There are two small mixed plantations and two areas of young oak planted in 1986. Management aims are to improve age structure by cutting and regeneration in selected areas, retaining valuable old and decaying trees, and to continue widening rides and creating glades. Operations consist of management of wide rides, maintenance of plantation and hazel coppice regeneration. Deer and woodland birds can often be seen. There are old woodland banks and areas of bluebells. National Trust shop in grounds of Mottifont Abbey (adjacent), and estate sawmill selling forest products.

Open: Free access at all times. Extensive rides. Public footpath. Car park closed 1st Nov.–1st Feb. each year.

---

11. THE HOLT
KINGSCLERE
Tel: (01993) 850224
SU567609

(Major R. A. Colvile)   68 ha. (170 acres)

From the B3051 S of Ashford Hill, take the road marked Wheathold.   From farm buildings (Cannon Stables) take track N (passable by cars when dry).

Mainly oak, fairly even aged. Poorest oak areas replanted 1966-1980, mainly with conifers but some poplar, red oak, cherry and nothofagus. Some natural regeneration of sallow, alder and ash. Ashford Hill Nature Reserve adjoins on the north side. As most of the wood is on clay, wellingtons or strong boots are advisable.

Open: Free access at all times. Extensive rides and paths. Public rights of way.

---

12. HOME FARM
BURKHAM
Tel: (01476) 581111
SU655417

(Woodland Trust)   137 ha. (338 acres)

From Basingstoke, follow the A339 S towards Alton for approximately 8 miles.   At the crossroads with Lasham and Bentworth, turn R towards Bentworth. Proceed up the hill, turn first R and then first R again.   Continue for approximately 1½ miles where the car park for Home Farm will be found on the L of the road.

Bus from Basingstoke to Bentworth, which is 1 mile S of Home Farm.   Nearest station is Basingstoke.

Home Farm was saved from the threat of becoming a waste tip through a magnificent donation to the Trust by Lord Sainsbury, which wholly funded the purchase of the site.   The farm consists of established woodland, newly planted woodland, and meadowland. It is a wonderful site to visit, with open views and numerous walking routes, and occasional benches.   Home Farm is a Woodland Creation Scheme site.

You can adopt an area of new woodland at Home Farm to commemorate events such as birthdays, weddings or whatever you may choose.

Open: Free access at all times. Wide rides through recently planted areas. 150 acres of open meadow as well as established woodland.

---

13. MILL COPSE
YARMOUTH
Tel: (01983) 882614
SZ357891

(Wight Nature Fund)   5 ha.   (12 acres)

Park in borough council car park off A3054 at Yarmouth. Walk along sea wall to old railway; turn R then L onto footpath to wood.

An ancient woodland site with small area of hazel coppice, home to bluebells, orchids, dormice. Rest of wood is mixed conifer plantation including coastal redwoods with clear felled areas being replanted with broadleaves. Bird hides allow views over Yar River and adjoining wet meadows. Management hopes to convert this plantation back to the splendour of a hazel coppice, typical of other west Wight woodlands.

Open: Free access at all times. Please keep to paths, to avoid disturbance to wildlife.

---

14. MORGASTON WOOD - THE VYNE
SHERBORNE ST. JOHN
Tel: (01256) 881337
SU625572

(National Trust)   63 ha. (156 acres)

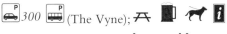300 (The Vyne);

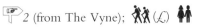2 (from The Vyne);

4 miles N of Basingstoke.   Take the A340 Aldermaston Road out of Basingstoke. Turn R into Morgaston Road.   Roadside parking.

Semi-natural oak woodland with some conifer plantations.   Coppicing of oak understorey in selected areas.   Variety of conifers, including larch, Scots pine, Douglas fir and Norway spruce.   Mature broadleaves and some old larch.   Wealth of archaeological features from Roman to 20th century.   Planting history closely linked with the Vyne House.   Wc's and refreshments at The Vyne (admission charge).

Open: Free access from dawn to dusk each day.   Extensive rides throughout wood.

---

15. THE NEW FOREST
LYNDHURST
Tel: (01703) 283141
SU300080

(Forest Enterprise)
26,500 ha.   (655,000 acres)

Between Southampton, Ringwood and Lymington.

Nearest station at Brockenhurst.

The finest example of multi-purpose forest management in the country, catering for such diverse interests as the growing of trees for timber, the pasturing of commoners' stock, the safeguarding of a biologically diverse ecosystem and the provision of facilities for recreation and education. The New Forest Museum and Visitor Centre in car park at Lyndhurst (not Forestry Commission) makes a good starting point (Exhibitions, audio/visual programme). A permissions system exists for field studies (prior arrangements with the Forestry Commission - at least 4 weeks' notice advisable).   Ranger-led activities/field studies - charges available on request.

Open: Free access at all times on foot.

---

16. OTTERBOURNE PARK WOOD
OTTERBOURNE
Tel: (01476) 581111
SU458223

(Woodland Trust)   24 ha.   (59 acres)

N of Eastleigh and Chandlers Ford. From the Chandlers Ford to Otterbourne road, turn into Boyatt Lane, past the Otter Inn. Park in Boyatt Lane and walk up Park Lane.

Buses run from Southampton to Otterbourne, just N of Otterbourne Park Wood. Nearest station is Southampton.

A semi-natural ancient woodland which has been designated as a County Heritage Site because of its long and interesting history and wealth of plants indicative of ancient woodland. Otterbourne is mentioned in the Domesday Book of 1086. In medieval times the village was split into two parts, one at the top of the hill and one in the valley. They were separated by Otterbourne Park, which was enclosed as early as 1253. Over the centuries the villagers have won a path through the wood, which still remains as a public footpath. The dominant tree species is the oak. A beautiful group of very old twisted and gnarled oak trees grows in the north of the wood. The oaks along the rides are Turkey oaks which were planted 50 to 60 years ago. Otterbourne Park Wood has a very rich ground flora. Flowers such as yellow pimpernel, yellow archangel and moschatel grow beneath the trees, whilst honeysuckle clambers up trunks and branches.

Open: Free access at all times. Public footpath and circular walks, along permissive paths.

---

17. PAMBER FOREST
TADLEY
Tel: (0118) 9700155
SU625605

(The Englefield Estate)
191 ha.   (478 acres)

Off A340 Basingstoke/Tadley road. Turn east at Pamber Green towards Bramley, then north to Little London and Silchester. At end of Little London, entrance is on L.

Bus - Along A340.

Large oak woodland with actively managed ride system and ancient ditch and bank system. An SSSI with very good invertebrate fauna, especially butterflies. Now managed by Hampshire Wildlife Trust. Management includes coppice restoration and grazed wood pasture.

Open: Free access at all times. Public rights of way and extensive ride system.

---

18. PARKHURST FOREST
NEWPORT
Tel: (01983) 522583
SZ480900

(Forest Enterprise)
395 ha.   (976 acres)

Take the A3054 Newport to Yarmouth road. Main entrance is beside two wooden houses, 2 miles from Newport.

Parkhurst Forest is a mixed broadleaved and conifer woodland. The forest was mentioned in the Domesday Book in the 11th century. It has diverse habitats, including mature oak, plantation conifer, coppice, heathland and wetlands. An excellent education service has been established to promote understanding of woodland management, conservation and sustainability. Nationally important forest for red squirrel conservation; squirrel viewing hide opening in 1998.

Open: Free access at all times. Extensive forest tracks and grass rides. Two waymarked walking trails and permitted horse route.

---

19. QUEEN ELIZABETH
COUNTRY PARK
PETERSFIELD
Tel: (01705) 595040
SU717182

(Managed by Forest Enterprise in partnership with Hampshire County Council)

600 ha. (1482 acres)

On A3, 5 mins. S of Petersfield and 15 mins. N of Portsmouth.

Bus along A3 ('phone Travel line 0345 023067)

Queen Elizabeth Country Park is part of the landscape of the South Downs and is in an Area of Outstanding Natural Beauty. The park is dominated by the three hills of Butser, War Down and Holt Down, which provide a contrast between the dramatic downland and beautiful woodland, predominantly of beech. Much of the park is a Site of Special Scientific Interest, and there are Iron Age and Roman sites.

Visitor centre with gift shop, refreshments, audio-visual theatre, activity area.

Bike hire, BBQ's for hire, events' programme, ranger service.

Open: Park open all year. Many statutory and permissive routes, for walking, riding and cycling. Visitor centre and cafe open 10.00-17.30/dusk every day April-Oct., weekends only Nov.-March. Disabled facilities.

Charges: Parking £1 per day Mon.- Sat.; £1.50 Sun. and bank holidays.

---

20. SELBORNE COMMON
SELBORNE
Tel: (01428) 683207
SU742335

(National Trust)   108 ha. (267 acres)

4 miles S of Alton between Selborne and Newton Valence, W of B3006. Zig zag path and woods are a short walk from car park in village.

Mature beech hanger woods on slopes above Selborne. Selborne Common is a large semi-natural wood of mainly beech and hazel, with some oak. Magnificent views over Selborne village. The woods are famous for their association with the pioneer 18th century naturalist, the Revd. Gilbert White, who spent many years observing and recording the natural history of the area.

Open: Free access at all times. Many tracks and paths.

---

21. SPEARYWELL WOOD
MOTTISFONT, NR. ROMSEY
Tel: (01794) 340757
SU315276

(National Trust)   22 ha. (55 acres)

Main entrance adjacent to B3084, approximately 4 miles N of Romsey.

Nearest station is Dunbridge.

The woodland consists mainly of plantations of various species, with fine stands of both hardwood and softwood planted between 1930 and 1960. Management aims are to continue good traditional silviculture to produce attractive woods and quality timber. Operations consist mainly of ongoing thinning and some planting. Deer and woodland birds can often be seen. There are old woodland banks and an area of bluebells under a stand of beech, which is a stunning sight when seen together with the early flush of the beech. National Trust shop in grounds of Mottisfont Abbey (adjacent) and estate sawmill selling forest products.

Open: Free access at all times. Unrestricted walking, and hard track surface suitable for prams/wheelchairs.

---

22. STONEY BROW
EAST TISTED, NR. ALTON
Tel: (01420) 588207
SU688304

(Sir James Scott Bt.)   72 ha.   (177 acres)

Duke of Cornwall's Award

1½ miles S of East Tisted on the A32, turn R for Borley. The wood is immediately either side of the public road.

Stoney Brow is a very varied woodland, with broadleaved and coniferous trees of all ages. It includes semi-mature oak and beech; sweet chestnut coppice growing on a 30 year rotation; 10 year old mixed hardwoods and conifers; 20 year old pure Norway spruce and Western hemlock; 25 year old Douglas fir; 40 year old mixed larch, oak and beech; 2 year old European larch in tree shelters; an area of natural scrubland with groups of natural regeneration of ash and birch; and an area of old mature broadleaves.

Open: Free access on foot at all times in daylight hours. Extensive rides and paths. No public right of way.

---

23. TOWN AND WALTERS COPSE
PORCHFIELD
Tel: (01983) 740956
SZ430905

(National Trust)   24 ha.   (60 acres)

Take the A3054 Yarmouth to Newport road. Turn L at Shalfleet Garage towards Porchfield. After about 1 mile, turn L to Newtown. Park in Newtown car park, with information point.

Bus - 35 - Porchfield

Town Copse is an oak wood with hazel understorey. Ω acre is coppiced annually and the oak standards are thinned. Walters Copse was meadows as recently as the 1920's. By coppicing ride sides we have encouraged a rich herb layer to return. Wildlife interest is excellent, including red squirrels, dormice and 35 species of butterfly. Spring displays of early purple orchid and primrose. Visitor point, bird hides, warden on site.

Open: Daylight hours, all year. Groups and schools by appointment only. Extensive ride network. Right of way.

---

24. WAGGONERS WELLS
HEADLEY
Tel: (01428) 683207
SU863344

(National Trust)   29 ha.   (72 acres)

Mature beech woodland, including some ancient pollards; and a series of picturesque man-made lakes.

Open: Free access at all times.

Why are the New Forest & Ashdown Forest not real forests?

The two best-known forests in the south east are as famous for their wild and windswept heaths as for their trees. Today, we expect a "forest" to be an extensive wooded area. But the New and Ashdown Forests are ancient forests, and when they were created some 900 years ago, the word had a very different meaning.

Forests for the King's sport

In Norman and medieval times, "forest" was a legal term, meaning land where the King (or other magnate) had the right to keep deer, and to impose forest laws to protect the deer. A forest was a place of deer, and only incidentally a place of trees. Forests were royal hunting grounds, and the deer that you see in the New and Ashdown Forests today are a reminder of the forests' original purpose.

In medieval times large areas of the south east were hunting forests. Ashdown Forest is said to have covered some 18,000 acres at one time (compared with 6,400 acres now);

Old print of deer hunting

with Waterdown and Dallington Forests to the east of it, and Worth and St. Leonard's Forests to the west, there was an almost continuous band of hunting forest across the High Weald in the Middle Ages.

The New Forest, together with the Forest of Dean in Gloucestershire, is the outstanding example of a surviving medieval English forest. It was established by William the Conqueror in about 1079. It still has its own Verderers' Court, which together with the Forestry Commission which now owns the forest, attempts to balance the age-old conflict between grazing and tree-growing.

From woodland to heath

Once these ancient forests were covered with trees, like the rest of south east England. The monarch had the right to fell trees for timber, and the commoners had the right to cut undergrowth. But as well as being royal hunting grounds they were (and still are) commons - places where local householders ("commoners") have rights to graze livestock. Deer and domestic livestock eat young seedling trees. As a result, the woodland could not regenerate, and gradually over the centuries great expanses of both forests became open heathland.

We cannot be sure what the forests looked like in the Middle Ages, but one of the greatest changes has been the reintroduction of the Scots pine in the 18th century. This tree quickly made itself at home, and is now one of the most familiar trees of the heaths of southern England.

Today, we appreciate these open heaths as wild places in a crowded and tamed part of the world. This is a recent viewpoint. William Cobbett, riding across Ashdown Forest in 1822, described it as "..... a heath, with here and there a few birch scrubs upon it, verily the most villainously ugly spot I ever saw in England".

Forests with a modern face

As for the other forests of the south east, most have entirely vanished, and in many cases even their names are forgotten. A few live on as forests in the modern sense - St. Leonard's Forest, for instance, and Alice Holt Forest on the Surrey/Hampshire border. Alice Holt nicely illustrates the changing role of forests through the centuries. Originally a Norman and medieval royal hunting forest, it had evolved into an important source of shipbuilding oak by the 18th century, and today is a Forestry Commission woodland park, growing mainly coniferous timber and giving pleasure to thousands of visitors each year.

1	Angley Wood
2	Bedgebury Pinetum
3	Blean Woods Nature Reserve
4	Bushy, Batfold & Kilnhouse Woods
5	Clowes Wood
6	Cutlers & Stanners Wood
7	Denge & Pennypot Wood
8	Hemsted Forest
9	Holly Hill Wood
10	Ightham Mote Woodlands
11	Joydens Wood
12	Kings Wood
13	Larkey Valley Wood
14	Oldbury Hill
15	One Tree Hill
16	Orlestone Forest
17	Parkwood
18	Scotney Castle Estate
19	Shoreham Woods
20	Shorne Wood Country Park
21	Stubbs Wood
22	Toys Hill
23	Trosley Country Park
24	Tudeley Woods

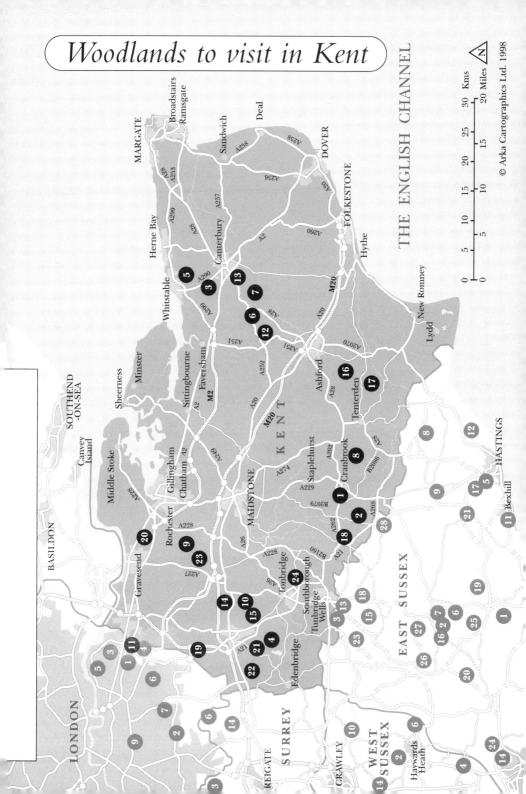

Woodlands to visit in Kent

© Arka Cartographics Ltd. 1998

1. ANGLEY WOOD
CRANBROOK
Tel: (01732) 870863
TQ768359

(Dr. R. Fitzwater)   124 ha. (307 acres)

The wood adjoins the A229 Cranbrook by-pass and the entrance is directly from the A229, approx. 300m. N of the junction with the B2189.

Bus stop at the entrance to the wood.

Angley Wood is a well established working woodland in the west Kent landscape. Tales going back to Elizabeth I and beyond record timber production, cloth making and a vengeful dragon. The principal species are Scots and Corsican pine and chestnut coppice, all of which are actively managed for their timber. Mature oak and beech are scattered throughout the wood. The area is a site of nature conservation interest with a number of less common woodland plants. It is also host to more than 30 species of breeding bird.

Open: Free access during daylight hours. Extensive ride and path network, including two public footpaths and one waymarked route.

2. BEDGEBURY PINETUM
GOUDEHURST
Tel: (01580) 211044
TQ715388

(Forest Enterprise)   120 ha. (297 acres)

Take the A21 N from Flimwell and after about 1 mile turn R on the B2079 to Goudhurst.

Bedgebury Pinetum is the National Conifer Collection and contains over 4,000 specimens representing 900 species and varieties of conifer. It is recognised as the best tree collection of its type in Europe. The Pinetum is an attractive place to visit at all times of year. In spring there are rhododendrons and azaleas in bloom and in September and October there are varied autumn colours. There is a great variety of fungi (protected) which are particularly abundant in autumn and uncommon birds, such as hawfinch and crossbill are regular visitors. Visitor centre, with information and shop (open 10.00-17.00, seasonal).

Open: All year, 10.00-17.00/dusk. Extensive rides and paths.

Charges: Adult £2.20; Child £1.20; OAP £1.70; Family £6.50.

3. BLEAN WOODS NATURE RESERVE
CANTERBURY
Tel: (01227) 462491
TR126592

(R.S.P.B.)   310 ha. (765 acres)

Centre of Excellence

Take the A290 Whitstable Road out of Canterbury, After 1½ miles, turn L into Rough Common; turn R after 500yds., following stone track for 500yds. to car park.

Buses 602, 603 and 605 from Canterbury to/near Rough Common.

One of the largest semi-natural broadleaved woodland reserves in Southern England, with extensive mature oak wood, plus managed coppice, rides, glades and heath. The wide range of breeding birds includes nightingale (about 30 pairs), redstart, wood warbler, tree pipit, kingfisher, nightjar and three species of woodpecker. One of the few remaining sites for the heath fritillary butterfly. Apart from annual coppicing, management includes conversion of some of the sweet chestnut coppice (poor in wildlife) to mixed coppice or high forest which will be richer in wildlife.

Open: Free access at all times on foot. 08.00 - 21.00 by car. Four waymarked paths.

---

4. BUSHY, BATFOLD AND KILNHOUSE WOOD
CHIDDINGSTONE
Tel: (01732) 463255
TQ505490

(Neil Wates Charitable Trust)
30 ha. (74 acres)

Take the B2027 which runs between Edenbridge and Tonbridge and follow the signposts to Bore Place.

Nearest station - Penshurst.

The woodlands are typical of the Low Weald, with oak and ash over an understorey of thorn, hazel and field maple. Mostly ancient woodland, and home to dormice, wild service tree, orchids and bluebells. The woodlands are being restored to coppice with standards and the wood is used sustainably with the aim of wasting nothing. Pea sticks through to milled oak is sold and a programme of coppice crafts is available using the wood for hurdle making, chair bodging, basketry, hedgelaying, etc.

Open: Free access at all times. Permissive paths.

---

5. CLOWES WOOD
CANTERBURY
Tel: (01580) 211044
TR137629

(Forest Enterprise) 241 ha. (596 acres)

From the A2 roundabout in Chestfield, take the minor road through Radfall towards Tyler Hill. The car park is on the R, 50 yards after a sharp L hand bend.

Clowes Wood is a mixed broadleaved/conifer woodland with a wide range of tree ages and sizes. The wood has many different habitats ranging from woodland, glades and ponds to grassy rides, which support a diverse range of flora and fauna.

Open: Free access at all times. Extensive rides and paths.

---

6. CUTLERS & STANNERS WOOD
CANTERBURY
Tel: 0181-883-4226
TR137629

(T. Reed) 56 ha. (138 acres)

8 miles SW of Canterbury on the A252, 2½ miles from junction with the A28.

An ancient mixed woodland and undulating topography, with some planting but also long periods of neglect, have produced a wide range of trees, shrubs and ground flora. The mammals, which include dormice and badgers, are equally diverse. A "no burning" policy to increase the humus content of the soil has increased fungal and insect diversity. These in turn have encouraged insectivorous birds. Prime timber and care for the environment are the present objectives.

Open: Free access during daylight hours. Pedestrian tracks only. No dogs.

---

7. DENGE AND PENNYPOT WOOD
CANTERBURY
Tel: (01476) 581111
TR105525

(Woodland Trust)   50 ha. (123 acres)

3

Turn off the A28 Ashford to Canterbury road to Shalmsford Street and Chartham. Follow the road through the village and take the right hand turning towards Thruxted. After ¾ mile turn L into Pennypot Lane towards Thruxted. Pennypot Wood is on the L after about 1 mile.

The structure of Denge Wood is varied, with a large area of sweet chestnut coppice. In other parts of the wood you will find a mixture of hazel and hornbeam coppice along with some fine yew and beech trees. Due to the mixture of habitats the wild flowers of Denge Wood, including bluebell, are a picture in spring and summer. The Warren, which is an area of shrubby grassland in the east of the wood, is one of the few places in Kent which supports a colony of Duke of Burgundy fritillary butterflies. Also around the area of the Warren you may hear the beautiful song of the nightingale.

Open: Free access at all times. Extensive network of rides.

---

8. HEMSTED FOREST
CRANBROOK
Tel: (01580) 211044

(Forest Enterprise)   397 ha. (981 acres)

30

From the crossroads at the W end of Benenden village, turn N towards Sissinghurst. Take the next R turn opposite the entrance to Benenden School. The entrance to the car park is on the L after about 500 yards.

A mixed broadleaved/conifer wood which was extensively damaged during the 1987 storm. It has been replanted over the subsequent years and there are still stands of excellent quality maturing Scots pine to be seen.

Open: Free access at all times. Extensive rides and paths.

---

9. HOLLY HILL WOOD
BIRLING
Tel: (01732) 876168
TQ670629

(Tonbridge & Malling Borough Council) 13 ha. (32 acres)

12

From the A228 just S of the M20 junction 4 at Leybourne, follow Park Road; turn R into Birling Road to Birling Village; turn R to Stangate Road, then L to Birling Hill. Follow signs to small car park.

Holly Hill Wood is an area of mixed broadleaved woodland of sweet chestnut with some ash, beech and oak. The chestnut was formerly managed as coppice. The wood is now managed to develop diversely structured high forest. There is a viewing point on high ground from which the Isle of Grain can be seen on a clear day. Bluebells are a feature in spring and interesting fungi are present in autumn.

Open: 08.00 – dusk. Circular path in wood and footpath through centre of wood.

---

10. IGHTHAM MOTE WOODLANDS
IVY HATCH
Tel: (01892) 890651
TQ585535

(National Trust)   16 ha. (40 acres)

100

3 miles S of Ightham, 6 miles E of Sevenoaks,

The estate surrounding the medieval Ightham Mote offers a variety of walks through farm and broadleaved woodland. The woodlands are rich in plant and animal life, bluebell and yellow archangel and red campion grow in profusion, and you may see Sika deer or dormice on your walk. Mote Farm is a working mixed arable and livestock farm.

Open: Free access all year, dawn – dusk. Waymarked paths. Disabled trail in Scathes Wood - key at ticket office.

---

11. JOYDENS WOOD
DARTFORD
Tel: (01476) 581111
TQ500720

(Woodland Trust)   137 ha. (339 acres)

Centre of Excellence

Travelling N on the M25, leave at junction 3 and go through Swanley on the B2173. Turn into Birchwood Road on the NW side of Swanley, then turn L into Summerhouse Drive. Park in Summerhouse Drive, with due regard to local residents.

A mixed conifer/broadleaf woodland currently in the thinning phase. Small area of heathland restoration. Some interesting archaeological features, notably Faesten Dic (Dyke), a Saxon frontier work dating back to AD814. Extensive walks provide an interesting variety of woodland flowers, including lily of the valley and Solomon's seal, and the red oaks provide a vivid splash of autumn colour.

Open: Free access at all times. Extensive waymarked routes marked on information boards at main entrances.

---

12. KINGS WOOD
ASHFORD
Tel: (01580) 211044
TR025500

(Forest Enterprise)   574 ha. (1418 acres)

Kings Wood is a predominantly broadleaved wood with extensive areas of sweet chestnut coppice. The wood has a sculpture trail situated just off the car park, which is run in partnership with the Stour Valley Arts Project.

Open: Free access at all times. Extensive rides and paths.

---

13. LARKEY VALLEY WOOD
CANTERBURY
Tel: (01227) 763763
TQ124557

(Canterbury City Council)
43 ha. (106 acres)

Take the A28 from Canterbury towards Ashford. Take first L after crossing over A2 and follow road round to R into Cockering Road. The car park is 1 mile on the L.

A mixed broadleaf woodland with beech, ash and oak dominating. The northern part is coppice, the south is high forest. Areas blown down in the 1987 storm are regenerating naturally. Eight species of orchid, nightingales and dormice present. One of the best places in Kent to see the hawfinch.

Open: Free access at all times. Extensive rides and paths.

---

14. OLDBURY HILL
SEVENOAKS
Tel: (01892) 890651
TQ582561

(National Trust)   62 ha.   (152 acres)

*24*

On the N side of the A25, 3 miles SW of Wrotham.

Buses along the A25 linking Seal to Borough Green.

Site of an Iron Age hill fort about 100BC. On a hilltop of the Greensand Ridge, with good views. Partly an ancient woodland site; largely acid sessile oak-birch woodland, with beech on the steep slopes. Fungal flora is particularly rich and remnants of heather can still be seen on this once lowland heath site.

Open: Dawn until dusk, all year. Many rights of way over the site.

---

15. ONE TREE HILL
SEVENOAKS
Tel: (01892) 890651
TQ560532

(National Trust)   14 ha.   (34 acres)

36

2 miles SE of Sevenoaks on the east side of Knole Park, betwen Underriver and Bitchet Common.

Site of Roman burials, this SSSI has fine views to the south.   The semi-natural woodland, badly affected by the 1987 storm, has restored itself naturally to achieve a structurally varied and uneven aged woodland. The only known British locality for the slug Tandonia rustica.

Open: Dawn until dusk, all year. Excellent footpath system, with the Greensand Ridge long distance footpath passing across this site.

---

16. ORLESTONE FOREST
ASHFORD
Tel: (01580) 211044
TQ986348

(Forest Enterprise)   451 ha.   (1114 acres)

20

From Ham Street village take the A2070 towards Ashford.   At the next crossroads (11/2 miles), turn L and then L again.   The car park is on the R, 50 yards beyond this junction.

Orlestone Forest has large areas of mixed broadleaved wood, with a scattering of coniferous trees.   The whole area is a designated SSSI and is well known for its lepidoptera and associated flora.

Open: Free access at all times. Waymarked walk.

---

17. PARKWOOD
APPLEDORE
Tel: (01303) 266327
TQ953316

(Kent County Council)   32 ha. (80 acres)

*25*

From Ham Street take the B2067 towards Tenterden,   turn L at T-junction towards Appledore. Parkwood is 1½ miles on L.

A mixed woodland with hornbeam coppice and oak standards.   Excellent wood for bluebells in the spring, white admirals and nightingale through the summer months. A peaceful and tranquil woodland site. BBQ charcoal from this wood is available.

Open: 09.00 – dusk. Waymarked paths.

---

18. SCOTNEY CASTLE ESTATE
LAMBERHURST
Tel: (01892) 890651
TQ688353

(National Trust)   317ha.   (783 acres)

1½ miles S of Lamberhurst, E of the A21, 8 miles SE of Tunbridge Wells.

The Scotney Castle estate offers a variety of paths through woodland and the parkland surrounding the famous landscape garden (admission fee). The parkland trees which are a mix of native and Victorian introductions, including monkey puzzle, were planted in the 1830s and 1840s. A SSSI covers most of the parkland, due to its unimproved plant-rich grassland, and ancient woodlands, because of their lichens and dead wood invertebrates. The woodland contains areas of sweet chestnut coppice and beech and oak plantations. The estate also contains a working hop farm and sheep and cattle.

Open: Free access all year, dawn - dusk. Waymarked paths.

---

19.   SHOREHAM WOODS
SHOREHAM
Tel: (01959) 534802
TQ501616

(Sevenoaks District Council)
101 ha. (250 acres)

Centre of Excellence

7 miles N of Sevenoaks off A224. Junction 4 off M25, take the A224 to Dunton Green. At next roundabout take first exit, Shacklands Road to Shoreham. Car park is 270 yds. on R.

Woods acquired from the Forestry Commission in 1991. Much of the woodland was damaged in the 1987 storm. The worst areas were cleared and replanted with mixed broadleaves. Much of the woodland is under 35 year old plantations of beech, oak and Norway spruce; also some chestnut coppice. An ancient woodland site with many features of interest. Ranger on site weekdays only.

Open: Free access at all times. Extensive rides and paths. Easy access path, including route for visually impaired.

---

20.   SHORNE WOOD
COUNTRY PARK
SHORNE
Tel: (01474) 823800
TQ684699

(Kent County Council)
70 ha. (174 acres)

Adjacent to the A2, between Gravesend and Rochester.   Take Shorne/Cobham turning (signposted from A2).

Buses - Strood/Meopham route.

Once part of Cobham Hall Estate, two thirds being ancient woodland, including old carriage rides with views over the Thames. The remaining third is an old clay extraction area, now transformed into meadows, ponds and woodland. An SSSI, particularly important for dragonflies. Arboretum, sensory garden, visitor centre and shop, adventure playground, BBQ's and fishing lakes. "Café in the Woods" open every day Easter - Sept., weekends in winter, 10.00–16.00.

Open: 09.00 - dusk, all year except Christmas Day.   Extensive path network. Easy access path.

Car parking charge: 50p Mon-Sat; £1 Sun. and Bank Holidays.

21. STUBBS WOOD

IDE HILL
Tel: (01732) 823570
TQ498518

(Kent County Council and Sevenoaks Borough Council) 40 ha. (99 acres)

½ mile E of Ide Hill along the B2042, turn R on to minor road at Y-junction. Parking 500yds. on R.

Bus via Sevenoaks on B2042.

Stubbs Wood lies on the top of the Greensand ridge with outstanding views of some of Kent's finest countryside. There are good well drained paths, but there are also some steep slopes. Much of the wood is managed chestnut coppice, with some mature oaks and beeches. An area of Scots pine was blown down in the 1987 storm; replacement trees are planted broadleaves and naturally seeded Scots pine.

Open: Free access at all times. Extensive paths, public rights of way and bridleway. Two circular walks.

22. TOYS HILL

BRASTED
Tel: (01892) 890651
TQ465517

(National Trust) 194 ha. (480 acres)

2½ miles S of Brasted, 1 mile W of Ide Hill. Car park close to the Fox & Hounds public house.

Highest point of Greensand Ridge in Kent, with magnificent views. The pollarded beechwoods on the acid-soiled plateau were 95% damaged in the 1987 storm. The more calcareous lower slopes have a varied flora, including lovely spring flowers, and were less damaged by the storm. The wood is an SSSI and contains heathland remnants and sessile oak woodlands with beech and birch. Excellent varied bird population. A 30 acre non-intervention zone has been left to monitor the woodland's natural succession process after the storm.

Open: Dawn to dusk, all year. Extensive rides and paths, with Greensand Ridge footpath crossing the woods. Disabled path.

23. TROSLEY COUNTRY PARK

MEOPHAM
Tel: (01732) 823570
TQ634612

(Kent County Council)
65 ha. (160 acres)

From the A227 follow signs to Vigo Village. Turn R into Waterlow Road and park is opposite.

Bus 308 along the A227.

Trosley Country Park includes mixed deciduous woodland on the crest of the North Downs. These ancient semi-natural woodlands contain fine yew 'tunnels' and pollarded hornbeams. The woodlands are managed to enhance their environmental and recreational quality. Coppicing is carried out with some of the timber being used to produce our own charcoal. There is an abundance of spring bluebells, and the woods are known for their rare violet helleborines. Fine panoramic views of the Weald below.

Visitor centre, special events in summer, observation hive with honey and wax produced.

Open: 08.30 - dusk. Closed Christmas Day. North Downs Way, public footpaths, right of way, bridleway.

Car parking charges: 50p weekdays, £1 Sunday and Bank Holidays.

---

24. TUDELEY WOODS
TONBRIDGE
Tel: (01273) 775333
TQ616433

(Mr. and Mrs. A.J.M. Teacher – R.S.P.B. Nature Reserve)   287 ha. (708 acres)

20   2

Centre of Excellence

Take the A21 S from Tonbridge. After 1 mile take minor road to Capel and turn L immediately before Shell garage. Car park is ½ mile on the L.

Nearest public transport Tonbridge / Tunbridge Wells.

Deciduous woodland on Tunbridge Wells Sand and Wealden Clay, comprising mature oaks with sweet chestnut and mixed coppice. Green, great-spotted and lesser-spotted woodpeckers are common and nuthatches abundant. Blackcap, garden warbler, willow warbler and nightingale inhabit the coppice. Hawfinch occurs annually, whilst hobby and nightjar breed occasionally. In spring, carpets of bluebell and primrose can be impressive. Seven species of orchid, including greater butterfly, bird's nest and violet helleborine, are found in the woodland.

Open: Free access at all times, except Christmas Day. Two waymarked visitor trails of 1½ miles and ¾ mile.

Why are trees being cut down?

The sound of chainsaws in the woods rings alarm bells in many people's minds, and none of us likes a favourite woodland scene being altered. But felling trees is part of the story of woodlands. In our crowded island, they have survived the farmer's axe only because they were (and are) a source of vital raw materials. Fortunately wood and timber are the perfect example of a renewable resource, so we have been able to harvest them for millennia without destroying the woodlands in the process.

Growing wood the old way

Walking in the winter woods, you may come across an area where all that remains is a sea of large stumps, with perhaps some scattered large trees, and stacks of cut poles. But by the following summer the stumps will have sprouted fresh green shoots, and after 15 years or so these will have grown into poles ready for cutting again. This ancient method of growing wood is called "coppicing", and is how almost all woods were managed until this century. Peer into almost any neglected wood in south east England and you will see the tell-tale multi-stemmed trees of old coppices, probably not cut for 40-50 years. Coppicing makes use of the tendency of broadleaved trees to resprout from the stump. In comparison, most coniferous trees cannot resprout and therefore cannot be coppiced.

Coppice poles were easily cut and moved by hand, and supplied materials for small buildings, fencing, tools, and above all for firewood and charcoal. Labour-intensive coppicing has all but vanished as wages have increased and markets have shrunk. The sweet chestnut woods of Kent and Sussex still find a fencing market, although that too has reduced in recent decades. Hazel coppicing in Hampshire is seeing a revival, supported by the County Council; the woven sheep hurdles made by hazel craftsmen are now too expensive for shepherds, but are popular with gardeners.

The Coppice Cycle

The trees are re-cut every 7-20 years, depending on the size of pole required.

Most broadleaved trees can be, and were, coppiced; but few conifers will resprout.

Timber for modern markets

Today, the main market is for long, straight timber trunks to be milled for rafters, planks and boards for the building trades; and this means coniferous trees. Small thinnings and poor quality material are used by the pulp industries for paper and board - or used to be, until recycled material took over much of this market. The hardwood timber from broadleaved trees is used for furniture and panelling, but this market demands top quality timber.

In woods being managed for timber, the trees are periodically thinned out to give the better ones enough light and space to grow large trunks. Thin too little and the good trees cannot develop; thin too much and the remaining trees may grow lots of side branches rather than a long straight trunk, and the wind may get into the wood and blow them over.

Eventually, the oldest trees are big enough to market for timber; at around 60 years for conifers such as pine, larch and Douglas fir and quick growing broadleaves such as wild cherry, but not until around 120 years for many broadleaves, including oak and beech.

Put back what you fell – and ask first

We have one of the most tightly regulated forestry industries in the world, with felling controlled by licences issued by the Forestry Authority. Woodland owners are normally obliged to replant with appropriate species, with the help of planting grants. In recent years the pendulum has swung against planting conifers on most existing woodland sites in the south east, although they are accepted in new woodlands if mixed with broadleaves.

The Plantation Cycle
Much simplified

PLANTING AND FENCING

WEEDING AND BEATING UP

THINNING (from 20 years)

FINAL FELLING (at 50 - 100 years)

Woodlands to visit in South London

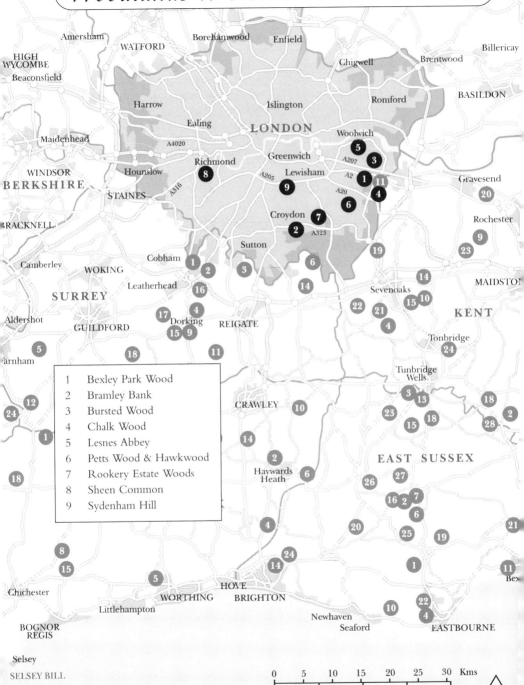

#	
1	Bexley Park Wood
2	Bramley Bank
3	Bursted Wood
4	Chalk Wood
5	Lesnes Abbey
6	Petts Wood & Hawkwood
7	Rookery Estate Woods
8	Sheen Common
9	Sydenham Hill

THE ENGLISH CHANNEL

| 0 | 5 | 10 | 15 | 20 | 25 | 30 | Kms |
| 0 | | 5 | | 10 | | 15 | 20 Miles |

N

© Arka Cartographics Ltd. 1998

1. BEXLEY PARK WOOD
BEXLEY
Tel: 0181-303-7777 (Extn. 4351)
TQ483738

(Bexley Council)   12 ha. (30 acres)

Take the A2 to Black Prince, then Bourne Road to Bexley Village High Street, then the B2210 Parkhill Road. Bexley Park Wood has four entrances: Camden Road, Parkhill, Elmwood Drive and Hurst Road.

Buses 229 and 269 along Parkhill Road. 20 min. walk from Bexley Village Station.

The wood is classified as a semi-natural ancient woodland and consists of mainly hornbeam coppice stools and mature oak. The wood had not been coppiced since before 1950. Coppicing was reintroduced in 1993 on a 30 year cycle. The woodland provides the shade, humidity and abundant dead wood for a large number of fungi to thrive. The flora of the wood includes many regionally rare species, including sanicle, hairy wood rush and pill sedge. Wide range of woodland birds, including three British woodpeckers. The nationally scarce ruddy darter dragonfly has also been seen in Bexley Woods.

Open: Free access at all times.

---

2. BRAMLEY BANK
SELSDON
Tel: 0171-261-0447
TQ352634

(London Borough of Croydon)
11 ha. (27 acres)

Main entrance is from Riesco Drive, off Ballards Way, South Croydon. Limited car parking in Riesco Drive.

Bus 130 to top of Gravel Hill (5 min.), or no. 64 along Addington Road, Selsdon. At least 25 minutes' walk from South Croydon Station.

Managed by London Wildlife Trust as a nature reserve, Bramley Bank almost links to the adjacent Littleheath Woods and, although parts are ancient, most has developed from former parkland. The woodland is composed of pedunculate oak, ash and sycamore, with Victorian plantings of Scots pine, sweet chestnut and beech. A large pond supports great crested newts, and an area of acidic grassland comprises heather, gorse and field woodrush.

Open: Free access at all times.

---

3. BURSTED WOOD
BEXLEYHEATH
Tel: 0181-303-7777 (Extn. 4351)
TQ499764

(Bexley Council)   12 ha. (30 acres)

Take the A220 from Bexleyheath towards Erith. Turn L immediately after crossing railway. Parking on R.

Several buses run nearby from Bexleyheath. Barnehurst Station ¼ mile.

Bursted Wood is predominantly sweet chestnut with oak standards. Local conservation volunteers actively participate in site work, including bramble clearance, to encourage wildflowers. The carpets of bluebells and wood anemones are a cherished feature of this woodland. Bird and bat boxes have been erected to supplement existing habitats, whilst coppicing has been reinstated within the last 10 years, having ceased about 60 years ago. The coppicing has involved leaving some sweet chestnuts as standards in order that this relatively small woodland maintains the "high canopy" atmosphere that local residents enjoy. Surplus timber has been used on a number of conservation projects within the Borough. The open area to the north of the woodland affords views towards the Thames and Essex. A sweet chestnut by the Swanbridge Road school entrance is known as "The Witches Face" - for reasons obvious to the visitor!

Open: Free access at all times.

---

4. CHALK WOOD
NORTH CRAY
Tel: 0181-303-7777 (Extn. 4351)
TQ494708

(Bexley Council)   26 ha. (64 acres)

Off the A223, heading S, turn L into Parsonage Lane. At top of lane, a dirt track leads to Chalk Wood. Track is not suitable for domestic vehicles.

Ancient ash/maple wood converted to sweet chestnut coppice. Forty two ancient woodland indicator species, including green hellebore and Solomon's seal. Winter roost of long-eared bats. At least 265 species of invertebrates identified, only a small number of total probably present. Two acidic meadows, one having Melampyrum pratense (common cow-wheat), a rarity in the London area. Hazel coppicing regime started in 1993/94.

Open: Free access at all times. Waymarked paths. Permitted bridlepath around perimeter.

---

5. LESNES ABBEY
ABBEY WOOD
Tel: 0181-303-7777 (Extn. 4351)
TQ478787

(Bexley Council)   88 ha. (217 acres)

600m. E of the centre of Abbey Wood on the B213. Off-site parking available in Abbey Road (B213) and New Road.

London Transport buses 99 and 409 pass the wood. Nearest station Abbey Wood.

These ancient semi-natural woodlands are mainly stored coppice with oak standards, but are very varied. The display of wild daffodils in early spring is famous throughout SE England. Bluebells and other flowers also abound. The woods contain a Victorian ornamental woodland pond and a remnant of the heathland which once covered Bexleyheath. There are picnic areas beside the formal gardens, and the ruins of a 12th century Augustinian abbey attract many visitors. The woods contain deposits of tertiary age fossils, and digging for fossil sharks teeth can be arranged by appointment. Information centre open 09.00 - dusk every day.

Open: Free access at all times.

---

6. PETTS WOOD AND HAWKWOOD
CHISLEHURST
Tel: (01892) 890651
TQ450687

(National Trust)   134 ha. (330 acres)

Park in Chislehurst and walk SE along the main A208. The woods lie to the SW of the road.

Petts Wood is so called after the Pett family who were royal shipbuilders from the time of Henry VIII to Charles II. William Willett, the founder of British Summer Time, who was an active Chislehurst resident, is commemorated in Willett Wood. Petts Wood and Hawkwood are ancient, semi-natural woods with predominantly oak and birch, and include several ponds. Rides are being widened, and bracken cut, as a precaution against fire. Neighbouring farmland is also accessible, under a Countryside Stewardship Scheme.

Open: Free access at all times. Many tracks and paths.

---

7. ROOKERY ESTATE WOODS
BROMLEY
TQ410664

(Rookery Estates Co.)   56 ha. (138 acres)

The woods are 1-2 miles S of Bromley High Street, bounded by Hayes to the W, Bromley Common to the E, and the Croydon Road to the S. Access is from any public road or path.

From Bromley Station, take bus to Orpington, alighting at Bromley Common

This is ancient woodland, all managed as coppice with standards. It is ecologically diverse, containing about eight stand types with large areas of two rare categories, lowland sessile oakwood and plateau alder. The flora is superb, including some 45 ancient woodland indicator species and 35 native trees and shrubs.   There are woodbanks, old pollards and an intricate natural drainage pattern as well as three miles of old rides and a rich bird life.

Open: Free access at all times.

8. SHEEN COMMON
EAST SHEEN
Tel: 0181-876-2382
TQ197745

(London Borough of Richmond)
21 ha. (52 acres)

Take the B351 Sheen Lane from Mortlake towards Richmond Park. Turn R into Fife Road.

Sheen Common has a fascinating history. Once a golf course and rifle range, it has now developed into a delightful woodland. Birch trees host nesting woodpeckers and a nature trail leads you to the pond with its dipping platform and lively frog population. Watch out for conservation projects which you can join in, helping to manage the woodland for wildlife, or book up to borrow the pond dipping/survey equipment. Ranger service.

Open: Free access, dawn to dusk, all year.

9. SYDENHAM HILL
UPPER SYDENHAM
Tel: 0181-699-5698
TQ344724

(London Borough of Southwark)   10 ha. (25 acres)

The main entrance is in Crescent Wood Road, SE26, which is off Sydenham Hill. This can be reached from either the A212 to the S at Crystal Palace, at the South Circular (A205) or to the N by the Horniman Gardens, Forest Hill, SE23. Limited car parking on Crescent Wood Road.

Bus route 63 (Crystal Palace to Kings Cross) stops right by Crescent Wood Road.

Managed by London Wildlife Trust, the wood is part of the largest surviving fragment of the historic Great North Wood – an economic resource for charcoal, timber and tannin. Today it exhibits the signs of its varied recent history - old Victorian gardens and an old railway trackbed.   Over 200 species of flowering plants are present, together with a multitude of fungi, birds and insects - notable species include all three woodpeckers, chiff-chaff, treecreeper, wild garlic and wood anemone under the dominant trees of oak, hornbeam, ash and yew. Declared a Local Nature Reserve in 1990. Many special events.

Open: Free access at all times.

Some trees of the South East

English and sessile oaks
(Quercus robur and Q. petraea)

- Known as the "Sussex weed", oak will grow in a very wide range of soils, from sandy heath to quite waterlogged clays; but to grow good timber it needs fertile, moist, heavy soils.

- Once of enormous importance for shipbuilding, and for tanning (using bark from coppice poles).

- Nowadays, good oak timber is used for furniture, high class joinery and veneers. The best trees can be very profitable, but a picturesque oak with heavy branches is useful only as firewood.

English oak

- Oak seedlings are rarely found in the shade of woodlands, but grow freely in the sunlight of abandoned fields. Grey squirrels do great damage to the bark of saplings.

- One of our most long-lived trees, it has more associated insect species than any other tree in Britain.

Beech
(Fagus sylvatica)

- A tree that grows on both the chalky soils of the Downs and the acid sands of the New Forest and High Weald.

- Popular as a plantation tree for several

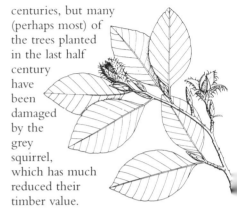

centuries, but many (perhaps most) of the trees planted in the last half century have been damaged by the grey squirrel, which has much reduced their timber value.

- Long straight trunks find a good market for furniture. Formerly it was a firewood and charcoal species, and pigs were turned out into beechwoods in the autumn to feed on the "mast" (nuts).

Sweet chestnut
(Castanea sativa)

- The fattest tree in England is a sweet chestnut; and the chestnut is as long-lived as the oak.

- Probably introduced by the Romans, it is a native of the Mediterranean. It has settled down happily on acid sands and loams in south east England, and forms natural woods with their own characteristics.

- Its rot-resistant poles used to be used in their thousands for the hop gardens of Kent and Sussex. It is still coppiced for fencing, although the market has shrunk recently.

- Its timber is similar to oak, and it should have a continued role as a timber tree on the right soils.

Hazel
(Corylus avellana)

- Although classified as a tree, it does not usually grow a single trunk, but tends to grow as a collection of poles even when not coppiced.

- It usually grows on damp but not waterlogged soils that are not very acid, and is the familiar coppice understorey in oakwoods.

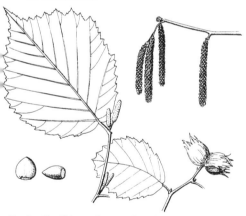

- Its flexible poles used to be an enormously important coppice crop, used for wattle in "wattle and daub" walls, sheep hurdles, fencing, thatching spars, barrel hoops, and of course firewood and charcoal.

- Nowadays, if hazel is cut it is generally for wildlife conservation rather than commercial reasons. However, the Wessex Coppice Group, centred on Hampshire, is leading a revival in hazel coppicing and coppice crafts, to meet

the growing market for "country-style" products for the home and garden.

Birch
(Betula pendula and B. pubescens)

- One of the commonest trees in the south east, birch grows particularly on acid heathy soils. A short-lived tree, with a healthy life expectancy of only 50-70 years.

- Birches produce millions of wind-borne seeds and is a very successful coloniser. A great deal of effort is spent removing birch saplings from around planted trees and from heathland.

- Although it is the basis of furniture, flooring and plywood industries in Scandinavia, there is almost no market for its timber here. Birch poles are used by turnery factories in Kent and Dorset, for brush handles.

Scots and Corsican pines
(Pinus sylvestris and P. nigra)

- Scots pine lived in southern England after the last Ice Age, but then apparently abandoned the south for Scotland. It was reintroduced into Surrey in the early 1600's, and to the New Forest in the late 1700's.

- Scots pinewoods are now a familiar

aspect of Surrey, Hampshire and Sussex heaths, on well-drained acid sandy and gravelly soils. It is little planted now, because it grows more slowly than alternative conifers, including Corsican pine.

- Its timber, known in the trade as deal or redwood, has been the standard utility timber of northern Europe for generations, for building and furniture.

- Like Scots pine, Corsican pine thrives in the comparatively dry south east, and on similar soils. It grows faster than Scots pine and therefore is more popular with timber growers.

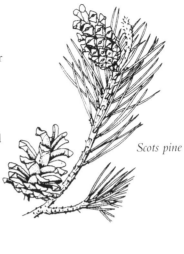

Scots pine

Corsican pine

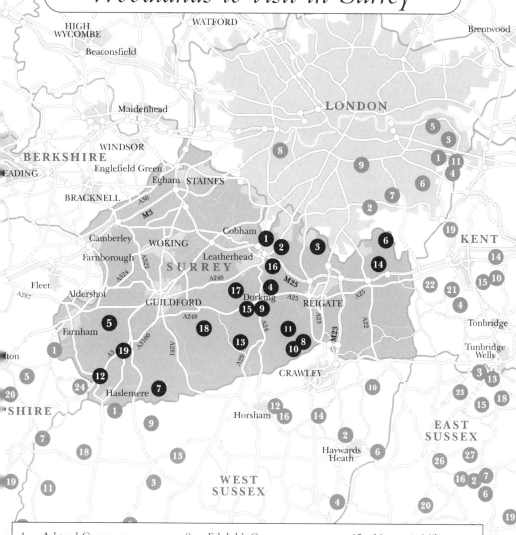

Woodlands to visit in Surrey

1	Ashtead Common	8	Edolph's Copse	15	Nower & Milton Heath, The
2	Ashtead Park	9	Glory Wood, The	16	Nower Wood
3	Banstead Woods	10	Glover's Wood	17	Ranmore
4	Box Hill	11	Hammond's Copse	18	Winterfold Forest
5	Britty Wood	12	Hindhead Woods	19	Witley Common
6	Crab Wood	13	Leith Hill		
7	Durfold Wood	14	Marden Park Woods		

THE ENGLISH CHANNEL

0   5   10   15   20   25   30 Kms
0   5   10   15   20 Miles   N

© Arka Cartographics Ltd. 1998

1. ASHTEAD COMMON
ASHTEAD
Tel: (01372) 279083
TQ180590

(Corporation of London)
200 ha. (500 acres)

Approaching Ashtead from the A24, turn L down Woodfield Lane opposite the Leg of Mutton and Cauliflower pub. Continue down the lane for 800m., straight over two mini roundabouts towards the railway station. Cross over the level crossing, and Ashtead Common lies in front of you.

Nearest station - Ashtead
(Horsham to Victoria/Waterloo)

First recorded history dates back to 1st century AD, the earliest evidence of human habitation being the remains of a Roman villa. Contains six major types of habitat; ancient pasture woodland, closed canopy woodland, bracken dominated areas, scrub grassland, semi-improved acid grassland, and several ponds. Designated a SSSI in 1955 and declared a National Nature Reserve in 1995. Pollarded oaks, birch and aspen. The various habitats support many species of invertebrates, together with a rich community of breeding birds, roe deer thriving in the woodland areas. Purple emperors and purple hairstreaks are amongst the numerous species of butterflies and moths.

Open: Free access at all times. Extensive network of public footpaths, bridleways and concessionary horse rides. Guided visits by appointment.
(please contact the Head Keeper on the above number).

2. ASHTEAD PARK
ASHTEAD
Tel: (01306) 879199
TQ192582

(Mole Valley District Council)
22 ha. (54 acres)

Leave cars in Ashtead village, on the A24; and reach the park from Rookery Hill on the N edge of the village.

Bus 479, Epsom to Ashtead.

Ashtead Park is situated on the heavy London clay and contains characteristic vegetation. It was once part of the park belonging to the Manor House at Ashtead, and the present park was laid out in the latter part of the 17th century. The park contains two main ponds and some fine specimen trees, as well as younger plantations. The park contains a wide variety of wildlife, and has been designated a Local Nature Reserve.

Open: Free access at all times. Extensive network of footpaths.

3. BANSTEAD WOODS
CHIPSTEAD/BANSTEAD
Tel: (01737) 276000
TQ273593

(Reigate & Banstead Borough Council)
115 ha. (284 acres)

Follow the B2219 (Holly Lane) from Banstead for 2 miles. Large car park on R.

Chipstead Station 300 yds.

Banstead Woods is an ancient woodland, possibly recorded in the Domesday Book. It has probably been woodland since the last Ice Age. The wood is a designated SSSI because of the rarity and variety of its flora which includes sessile oak and some very old coppice woodland.

Open: Free access at all times. Extensive permissive footpaths, public rights of way round outside. Nature trail with leaflet (tel. 0181 541 7282).

---

4. BOX HILL
DORKING
Tel: (01306) 885502
TQ171519

(National Trust)   217 ha. (536 acres)

Centre of Excellence

On the A24, 1 mile N of Dorking, 2½ miles S of Leatherhead. Coaches must not use zig zag road from Burford Bridge on W side of hill.

Bus - London and Country 516. Box Hill and Westhumble Station ½ mile.

An outstanding area of woodland and chalk downland. Many beautiful walks and views towards South Downs. Semi-natural beech, yew and box with some areas of open downland. Visitor centre, souvenirs, refreshments, special events.

Open: Access at all times. Extensive paths and rides. Public rights of way.

Car parking charge £1.50 (non-NT members).

5. BRITTY WOOD
FARNHAM
Tel: (01483) 810208
SU900454

(Trustees of the Hampton Estate)
60 ha. (148 acres)

S of the A31 and W of the A3.

The woodlands are situated on light sandy soil and walking is easy at all times. Extensive views to the south. There is a variety of woodland, including plantations of pine and larch approximately 30-40 years old and oak 80 years old. The woods are thinned in rotation and provide a habitat for a variety of birds.

Open: Free access at all times. Rides and paths. One public footpath.

---

6. CRAB WOOD
BIGGIN HILL
Tel: (01883) 623038
TQ390600

(J. Bothamley)   28 ha. (69 acres)

From Farleigh Common (on road between Warlingham and Selsdon) take Farleigh Court Road (brick pillar box) for ¾ mile to "Newlands Barn".

Semi-ancient mixed woodland. Some very old ash coppice and actively worked chestnut coppice (1 ha.). New mixed planting on 2 ha. in 1995. Several very large beech trees. A quiet mixed woodland with acres of bluebells and, since 1994, deer.

Open: Free access at all times.

---

7. DURFOLD WOOD
DUNSFOLD
Tel: (01428) 581111
SU992330

(Woodland Trust)   16 ha. (43 acres)

From the A283 at Chiddingfold, take minor road toward Hazel Bridge. After 2 miles turn L into Fisher Lane. Durfold Wood is on the R after 1 mile.

The wood contains a variety of broadleaved trees. Open areas have patches of bilberry and heather. A SSSI, as this wood forms part of a large area of oak woodland. A good site for birds, including woodcock, nightingales, lesser spotted woodpecker and sparrowhawk.

Open: Free access at all times. Extensive rides and paths. Public right of way.

---

8. EDOLPH'S COPSE
CHARLWOOD
Tel: (01476) 581111
TQ235424

(Woodland Trust)   27 ha. (68 acres)

From Charlwood village, take Stanhill Road towards Newdigate. Parking is ½ mile on R hand side.

A matrix of woodland types of varying ages. High forest and hazel coppice under management. Three ponds, unimproved meadow and open scrubby area. Wild service trees, small leaved lime, violet helleborine. Management includes ride side widening and hazel coppicing on rotation.

Open: Free access at all times. Extensive rides and paths.

---

9. THE GLORY WOOD
DORKING
Tel: (01306) 879199
TQ171487

(Mole Valley District Council)
12 ha. (30 acres)

From the W end of Dorking High Street, take the path from Chequers Yard S to St. Pauls School and beyond until you reach the woods.

Buses/trains to Dorking town centre.

This fine woodland is situated on the sandstone hills south of Dorking, and contains a wide variety of trees, particularly beech. The southern section, known as the Devil's Den, supports mainly oak, with sweet chestnut coppice. Parts of the site were badly damaged in 1987, and clearance and replanting is still going on. The Glory Wood was given to the former Dorking Council by the Duke of Newcastle in 1929.

Open: Free access at all times. Extensive footpaths, including rights of way. Greensand Way crosses the wood.

---

10. GLOVERS WOOD
CRAWLEY
Tel: (01476) 581111
TQ228407

(Woodland Trust)   27 ha. (67 acres)

The S end of the wood is adjacent to the minor road "Russ Hill". The village of Charlwood is situated W of the M23 near the junction of the A217 and A23 London to Brighton road at Hookwood. Park in Glover's Road in Charlwood and follow public footpath to wood.

Buses to Charlwood.

Partly ancient woodland, lying along a "ghyll" (stream). Partly newer woodland where former field boundary banks can still be seen. Coppicing is being reintroduced in part, and other areas are being selectively thinned so that remaining trees grow up into high forest. A SSSI because of its ghyll woodland, and because it is the largest Wealden woodland on Paludina limestone (sometimes known as "Sussex marble"). Trees include small leaved lime and Wych elm, which are rare in the Weald.

Open: Free access at all times.

11. HAMMOND'S COPSE
PARKGATE
Tel: (01476) 581111
TQ209443

(Woodland Trust)   30 ha. (73 acres)

From Parkgate, take minor road N (Broad Lane) towards Brockham. Parking is 300m. on R.

Part semi-natural ancient woodland (oak woodland and hazel coppice) and part ancient woodland (conifer plantations). Pond in centre of wood. Bluebells and dog's mercury are abundant. Coppicing of hazel recently reintroduced.

Open: Free access at all times. Extensive rides and paths. Several public rights of way.

12. HINDHEAD WOODS
HINDHEAD
Tel: (01428) 683207
SU892357

(National Trust)   500 ha. (1235 acres)

12 miles SW of Guildford on both sides of the A3 (Portsmouth Road). Main car park is 400m. N of Hindhead traffic lights.

Bus - Tel. Guildford Bus Station (01483) 575226. 2 miles from Haslemere Station.

Extensive areas of Scots pine, oak and birch woodland with areas of open heath. Good walks and extensive views. Refreshments.

Open: Free access at all times. Extensive rides and paths. Public rights of way.

13. LEITH HILL
COLDHARBOUR, DORKING
Tel: (01306) 711777
TQ132428

(National Trust)   270 ha. (666 acres)

NW of the A29; W of the A24; S of the A25.

Well managed productive woodland, with areas of ancient semi-natural woodland. Extensive views. Bluebells and rhododendrons. Refreshments (April - Sept).

Open: Free access at all times. Extensive rides and paths. Public rights of way.

Car parking charge at Rhododendron Wood: £1.50

14. MARDEN PARK WOODS
CATERHAM
Tel: (01476) 581111
TQ370540

(Woodland Trust)   62 ha. (153 acres)

From the M25, junction 6, take the A22 N towards Croydon. Turn R (signed Woldingham) and bear R into village. Continue through village and turn R along Gangers Hill. Entrance to wood approximately 150 yds. on R after sharp bend.

Marden Park is situated within the Surrey Hills AONB. It comprises three areas of woodland: the Old Rifle Range, Stubbs Copse, (including The Rumps) and Horse Shaw. The wood is part ancient semi-natural woodland, with pockets of rich chalk grassland where salad burnet and quaking grass can be found. Also, if you look carefully you may come across common spotted orchids in early summer. There is a wide variety of trees, including oak, ash, beech and field maple. These woods are home to a variety of wildlife, including tawny owls, roe deer, three types of woodpecker, rare Roman snails and striped-winged grasshoppers.

Open: Free access at all times. Extensive rides shown on information board in car park.

15. THE NOWER AND MILTON HEATH
DORKING
Tel: (01306) 879199
TQ155490

(Mole Valley District Council)
36 ha. (89 acres)

 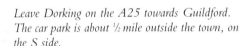

Leave Dorking on the A25 towards Guildford. The car park is about ½ mile outside the town, on the S side.

Buses/trains to Dorking town centre.

The area is sandy heathland and woodland, with an open grass area at the E end. The woodland includes native broadleaves, plus groups of young conifers planted in recent years. Areas of silver birch have been cleared to encourage bluebell regeneration. The high ridge which runs along the southern boundary affords fine views over the Weald to the south, and northwards across Dorking to Ranmore and Box Hill.

Open: Free access at all times. Extensive network of footpaths and public rights of way. On Greensand Way long distance path.

16. NOWER WOOD
LEATHERHEAD
Tel: (01372) 379509
TQ193546

(Surrey Wildlife Trust)   33 ha. (82 acres)

From junction 9 of the M25, follow signs to the A24 and join it southbound. Turn off at first exit (Beaverbrook roundabout) on to the B2033. Entrance on the L after 1 mile.

Nower Wood is 81 acres of mixed woodland, mainly broadleaved, with 40 different tree and shrub species. Over 70 species of birds have been seen in this ancient woodland, many of which breed on site. There are also areas of marshland, heath and chalk grassland, and several pools and ponds. The Surrey Wildlife Trust purchased Nower Wood in 1971 and gradually established it as an educational nature reserve. Field centre. Refreshments on open days.

Open: Public open days 3rd Sundays, April - October, 11.00 - 15.30. School and group visits by appointment, all year. Access for disabled.

Charges: Open days: Adult £1. Booked schools and groups: telephone for details.

17. RANMORE
DORKING
Tel: (01306) 742809
TQ142504

(National Trust)   266 ha. (658 acres)

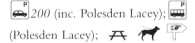

(Polesden Lacey);

2 miles NW of Dorking on unclassified road (Dorking-East Horsley) (Also adjacent southern boundary of Polesden Lacey Estate - approached from Bookham on the A246 (Leatherhead-Guildford road), 11/2 miles from Bookham.)

Extensive wooded common – mostly semi-natural oak, ash and birch with various managed plantations. Adjacent to southern boundary of Polesden Lacey Estate (N.T.) Polesden Lacey Estate walks include routes through Ranmore Common. Guide leaflet available at Polesden Lacey car park. (Facilities at Polesden Lacey Estate April-end Oct. (exc. Mon & Tues). Weekends March & Nov. Charge for park and gardens £3.)

Open: Free access at all times. Extensive rides and paths. Public rights of way.

---

18. WINTERFOLD FOREST
FARLEY GREEN/SHERE
Tel: (01483) 203474
SU065435

(J.A.C. McAllister)   135 ha. (350 acres)

Centre of Excellence

From the A254 Guildford to Dorking road, take the A248 (signposted Godalming). After ½ mile cross small bridge, then turn L into New Road up hill over level crossing to Farley Green, then L at village green into Shophouse Lane, then 1 mile to forest sign.

Densely planted working forest in the Surrey Hills (highest point of SE England), with 23 different species of tree – Corsican pine, Douglas fir, cypress, larch, Japanese cedar, etc. Wildlife includes deer, badger, fox and snakes. Many species of bird, including birds of prey. Herd of tame Sika deer. Heathland recreation project in hand.

Open: Free access by booking/telephoning in advance. Great variety of access to suit all types. Good access for disabled.

19. WITLEY COMMON
WITLEY
Tel: (01428) 683207
SU933407

(National Trust)   152ha. (376 acres)

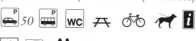

7 miles SW of Guildford between the A3 and the A286. 1 mile SW of Milford.

Bus - Stagecoach Hants and Surrey/Coastline , Guildford-Bognor Regis route.

2 miles from Milford Station.

Mixed age Scots pine, and lowland heath, with varied and interesting wildlife. Visitor centre, souvenirs (open April-end Oct). Special events.

Open: Free access at all times. Extensive rides and paths. Public rights of way.

After the storm - 12 years on

On the night of 16th October 1987 the cosy south east of England was unexpectedly hit by a violent windstorm. This was an unforgettable night for the people of the region, accustomed to a calm uneventful climate, and believing that such events only happened in exotic locations such as the Caribbean.

The trees and woods of the region were no more used to such winds than its inhabitants, and dawn brought a scene of devastation. No-one really knows how many trees were lost, but the total has been estimated at 15 million. Some were uprooted (and in some cases carried several metres by the wind), and with others the trunk was snapped like a twig. Countless trees lost major branches from the crown.

Because the storm was at night, few people were killed. But because it happened in the autumn, when deciduous trees were still clad in leaves, far more trees were damaged than if it had been a winter storm. Wind speeds of over 100 mph are much more usual in the north and west of Britain; therefore their trees have adapted to high winds, whereas the trees of the south east are more vulnerable to strong gales. It was often the inside of a woodland that was devastated in 1987, leaving a fringe of wind-firm edge trees. Trees inside a wood are accustomed to protection from their neighbours, but as soon as the wind fells a group of them, the rest are vulnerable.

Just how unusual was the storm?

No-one could remember anything like it, but meteorologists soon reassured us that such wind speeds could be expected every 200 years or so. A terrible storm hit southern England on 26th November 1703. Thousands of people were killed, and the Royal Navy lost an entire fleet; the worst disaster in naval history. John Evelyn, the silviculturalist and diarist, described the damage to trees: ".....that late dreadful hurricane subverted so many thousands of goodly oaks, prostrating the trees, laying them in ghastly postures, like whole regiments fallen in battle ......"

If such a terrible storm recurs every couple of centuries, that is well within the lifespan of many of our trees, such as oak, sweet chestnut and yew. It is quite a "normal" event for a woodland.

Reaction to the storm

Amazement and awe; insecurity in the face of such a change to our familiar surroundings; grief at the loss of treasured trees and landscapes; these were some of our initial personal reactions.

Different kinds of storm damage in woodland

swathe of damage   crown damage   canopy gap

Then the business of clearing up began. Chainsaw gangs from all over the country moved into the south east to help with the work. The Countryside Commission set up "Task Force Trees" to channel funds to local authorities and voluntary bodies. This began as a six month programme, but ran for 6½ years. The Forestry Commission co-ordinated a Forest Windblow Action Committee to help woodland owners with clearance and marketing of timber, and the government added a special "storm supplement" to replanting grants, acknowledging the extra cost of harvesting shattered woodlands.

A widespread initial response was to remove all signs of the storm as quickly as possible from public places - clear fallen trees, grind out the stumps, grass over the scars, plant new ones. Perhaps this was partly because we found it hard to accept that the storm was a natural process, and tended to blame our own tree management for the devastation. If old trees blew over we blamed ourselves for not replacing them sooner, and if young plantations blew over we blamed ourselves for planting "unnatural" woodlands!

In retrospect, it is perhaps regrettable that all signs of the storm have been erased from so many public places; it was, after all, one of the most memorable events in the recent history of the south east.

Many woodlands have now been cleared up and replanted. In most cases this will have been a great financial burden to the owner. Market prices were depressed by the glut of timber flooding the market; the cost of retrieving any marketable timber from the tangle of trees was very high; and in many woodlands the trees had not yet grown to a marketable size.

However, many fallen trees have not been cleared. You can still peer into neglected woods and see horizontal giants amongst the undergrowth that has sprung up in the increased sunlight. In many cases the horizontal trees are still alive, and natural regeneration in time will fill the gaps. We like quick results, and to impose control and tidiness on our surroundings. But twelve years is insignificant in the life of an oak or beech tree, or the history of a woodland.

Woodlands to visit in West Sussex

1 Blackdown Wood
2 Borde Hill Gardens
3 Burton Pond Woodlands
4 Butcher's Wood
5 Clapham Woods
6 Costells Wood
7 Durford Wood

8 Eartham Wood
9 Ebernoe Common Nature Res
10 Gravetye
11 Harting Down Local Nature Res
12 Leechpool & Owlbeech Woods

13 Mens Nature Reserve, The
14 Nymans Wood
15 Slindon Woods
16 St Leonard's Forest
17 Stansted Forest
18 Woolbeding Wood

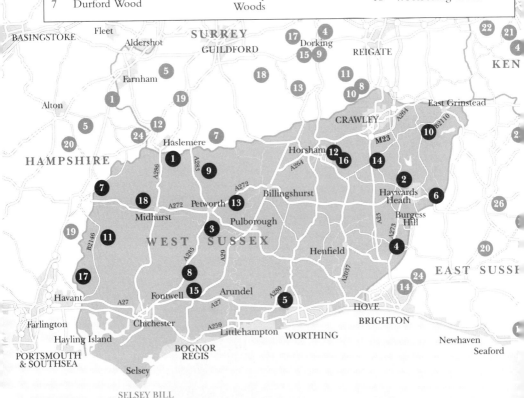

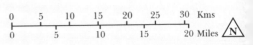

© Arka Cartographics Ltd. 1998

1. BLACKDOWN WOODS
HASLEMERE
Tel: (01428) 683207
SU920308

(National Trust)   303 ha. (749 acres)

1 mile SE of Haslemere

Extensive Scots pine, oak and birch woodlands on sandy heath, with attractive walks.

Open: Free access at all times.

2. BORDE HILL GARDENS
(WARREN WOOD, STEPHANIE'S GLADE AND STONE PITTS)
HAYWARDS HEATH
Tel: (01444) 450326
TQ322262

(Mr. and Mrs. A.P.J. Clarke)
81 ha. (200 acres)

1½ miles N of Haywards Heath on the Balcombe Road.

Haywards Heath Station 1 mile.

Three separate woodlands in spectacular Sussex parkland and garden. Each wood comprises magnificent specimen trees. They include many varieties, with over 400 Acers, 370 oaks, 200 firs and Abies, and some of the tallest pines in this country. Borde Hill contains Britain's largest number of Champion trees in a private collection. The woods are a delight in the spring with rhododendrons and bluebells, cool and peaceful in the summer months, turning fiery in the autumn. Blooms of Bressingham plant centre. Visitor centre being built in 1998/99 from recently awarded Heritage Lottery Grant. Refreshments.

Open: 10.00 – 18.00 every day of the year. Several marked paths of different length.

Charges: £3 adults; £1.50 children.

3. BURTON POND WOODLANDS
PETWORTH
Tel: (01273) 492630
SU978181

(Sussex Wildlife Trust)   27 ha. (67 acres)

Head S from Petworth on the A285. After about 2 miles, just over the brow of the hill beyond a garage, take the second L (signposted Burton Park). Burton Pond is about 1 mile from the A285.

The reserve consists of woodlands enclosing areas of bog and surrounding a large mill pond. The woodlands - Newpiece Wood, Welch's and Crouch Common, and the Warren - all derive from oak and birch woodlands, though much altered in the past. There are many heathy areas and the Black Hole - a bog on Welch's Common, now partly covered by alder and willow – supports plant species more usually associated with the north and west of Britain. In the drier woodlands, birch has spread into the areas where the felling of oak and lime was once common. Some of these birch blocks have been replaced with a more natural mix of broadleaved trees, including oak. The mill pond is a good place to see wildfowl. The woodlands are part of Burton and Chingford Ponds Local Nature Reserve.

Open: Free access at all times, along rides and paths.

4. BUTCHER'S WOOD
HASSOCKS
Tel: (01476) 581111
TQ304153

(Woodland Trust)   8 ha. (19 acres)

Park at Hassocks Railway Station. Follow footpath S next to railway line until you reach entrance to wood on the L.

Bus to Hassocks.

Located just north of the South Downs, in the Sussex Downs AONB. Semi-natural ancient woodland with a wide age range and structure, including oak high forest and hazel coppice. A small meadow and stream on the eastern part of the wood. Hazel coppicing cycle is carried out by a local community group. Great bluebell wood in the spring.

Open: Free access at all times. Extensive rides and paths creating circular routes around the wood.

---

5. CLAPHAM WOODS
CLAPHAM
Tel: (01903) 264686/830355
TQ105059

(J. F. and C. C. Somerset)
145 ha. (358 acres)

Off the A27 Arundel to Worthing road. The drive to Holt Farm House is on the N side of the road, opposite Castle Goring to the W and the Coach & Horses public house to the E.

2 miles from Goring Station.

Semi-natural ancient woodland. Primroses, bluebells and wood anemones grow beneath hazel, with oak and ash standard trees. In 1989 a blanket Tree Preservation Order prevented any coppicing or cutting. Coppicing was resumed in 1996 following a woodland management agreement with the Forestry Authority. New trees are being planted in the coppiced areas to provide standard trees at a density of 50 trees per hectare in the future.

Open: By appointment only, in daylight hours, April and May.

---

6. COSTELLS WOOD
SCAYNES HILL
Tel: (01476) 581111
TQ370235

(Woodland Trust) 53 ha. (21 acres)

From Haywards Heath, follow the A272 E towards Scaynes Hill. At Scaynes Hill turn L into village (Church Road). Parking at Scaynes Hill Common.

Bus to Scaynes Hill on A272.

Mixed broadleaved woodland with open areas where heather can be found. There are three ponds and two streams which have created steep ghylls. Management involves reintroducing coppicing of hazel and ride widening to create glades. Plant species include hemlock, water figwort, forget-me-not, yellow archangel, wood anemone, bluebells and lesser spearwort.

Open: Free access at all times. Extensive rides and paths. Public footpath from Scaynes Hill Common.

---

7. DURFORD WOOD
ROGATE
Tel: (01730) 816638
SU799260

(National Trust) 26 ha. (64 acres)

From The Jolly Drovers public house on the ol A3, head E towards Rogate. Car park is 40 yards on the R.

Durford is a varied site comprising old oa coppice, Scots pine woodland and heathland understorey. The mos remarkable feature of the small property is i ability to "swallow" visitors - however bus the little car park gets, the visitor can always experience solitude. National Trust management is focused on nature conservation and quiet enjoyment.

Open: Free access, dawn to dusk, all year. Access via Sussex border path and various permitted routes.

---

8. EARTHAM WOOD
CHICHESTER
Tel. (01420)23666
SU936106

(Forest Enterprise, leased from the National Trust)   260ha. (642 acres)

 30

From Chichester, take the A27 E. After about a mile turn left onto the A285 to Petworth. Take the second turning to the R signed Eartham; the car park is 200 m. on the L.

The woodlands are predominantly beech planted in 1950-5, with a few small areas of conifers. There are numerous paths, most of which provide easy walking and are usually dry underfoot due to the chalky underlying rock. Running from south-west to north-east is Stane Street, a fine example of a Roman road, which once linked Chichester with London.

Open: Free access at all times, but please note that there is an area adjoining the west of the wood which is privately owned and not open to the public (fenced off and signed).

---

9. EBERNOE COMMON
NATURE RESERVE
NORTHCHAPEL
Tel: (01273) 492630
SU976278

(Sussex Wildlife Trust)   72 ha. (178 acres)

 9

Take the A283 N from Petworth. After about 3 miles, take the minor road R (first road outside the town). Follow this winding road until you reach a red phone box. About 10 yds. further on the R the entrance is marked "Ebernoe Church".

Ancient woodland with grassy glades, ponds and archaeological remains. Once wood pasture for commoners' livestock. Ebernoe has huge oak and beech trees, with holly shrub undergrowth, as well as an old furnace pond and a brick kiln - a scheduled ancient monument. There is also an outstanding "unimproved" flower rich meadow. The diverse habitats give rise to over 300 species of plants, 100 of mosses and 400 of fungi, many of the latter flourishing on dead and dying timber. Pond clearance, and the removal of bracken and holly from glades and rides, are annual tasks in parts of the reserve. It is hoped grazing will be reintroduced. The woodland areas are deliberately left to continue a natural cycle of growth and decay.

Open: Free access at all times, along rides and paths. Take care not to get lost - we strongly advise you keep to paths.

---

10. GRAVETYE
EAST GRINSTEAD
Tel: (01420) 23666
TQ36034

(Forest Enterprise)   316 ha. (781 acres)

 15

From Turner's Hill, take the B2028 SE for approximately 1 mile. Turn L towards Sharpthorne, and L again into Vowells Lane. Car park is on the R, 500 yards beyond the entrance to Gravetye Manor.

Gravetye is a very mixed woodland in terms of both tree species and ages. The area was once part of a private estate and has small areas of farmland amongst the woodlands. Please use the rights of way when crossing these. The woods have many tracks and paths within them, but the clay soils mean that stout footwear may be needed after wet weather.

Open: Free access at all times.

---

11. HARTING DOWN LOCAL
NATURE RESERVE
SOUTH HARTING
Tel: (01730) 816638
SU790180

(National Trust)   240 ha. (600 acres)

Entrance to car park is adjacent to the B2141, approximately 1 mile S of South Harting village.

As the name suggests, this property is predominantly chalk grassland. However, it includes areas of woodland which are open to the public. These woods range from wood pasture with old beech pollards to younger woods of ash and hazel. Dog's mercury, ransoms and dog violet are just a few of the ground flora species to be found. As the National Trust's management encourages old "veteran" trees, with lots of deadwood, the woods are home to fauna such as bats, woodpeckers and owls.

Open: Free access dawn to dusk, all year. There are rights of way within the woods and the public has the freedom to roam.

---

12. LEECHPOOL AND
OWLBEECH WOODS
HORSHAM
Tel: (01403) 256890
TQ194314

(Horsham District Council)
34 ha. (85 acres)

To the E of Horsham town centre just off the B2195 (Harwood Road).

Mixed woodland, pine forest and heathland which can be explored by two self-guided walks of 1 and 2 miles. There is also an orienteering course of intermediate standard covering both woods. Blocks of sweet chestnut are being recoppiced for the first time since the 1930's, and an area of Owlbeech Woods destroyed by fire some years ago is gradually being recolonised by heather.

Open: Free access at all times. Extensive network of footpaths. Two waymarked trails. "Easy-going" trail for wheelchairs.

---

13. THE MENS NATURE RESERVE
PETWORTH
Tel: (01273) 492630
TQ023237

(Sussex Wildlife Trust)
159 ha. (393 acres)

Take the A272 E from Petworth. After about 4 miles, turn R at crossroads in the middle of a large wood, signposted Hawkhurst. Car park is about 100 yards on R.

A superb ancient beech and oak woodland with medieval woodbanks and "assarts" (clearings). The Mens is unusual in not having been in management for decades, and is reverting to the nature of a "wildwood". The mass of fallen timber and old trees supports numerous rare deadwood fungi, beetles and other species. The reserve includes a number of unimproved flower rich meadows.

Open: Free access at all times, along rides and paths.

---

14. NYMANS WOOD
HANDCROSS
Tel: (01444) 400321
TQ264295

(National Trust)   76 ha. (188 acres)

On the B2114 at Handcross, just off the London to Brighton (M23/A23) road.

Mature broadleaved woodland with areas of younger planted woodland.   Some fine specimen trees.   Waymarked woodland walks. Visitor facilities (shop, restaurant, information, wc's) available at Nymans Garden. Entrance fee to garden.

Open: Free access at all times.

---

15. SLINDON WOODS
SLINDON
Tel: (01243) 814554
SU952073

(National Trust)   550 ha. (1359 acres)

On the A27 N from Chichester, take the first turning on the L after the Fontwell roundabout. Car park is 200m. along on the R. Second car park is on top of Bignor Hill.

Highly varied mix of species and structure, due to the 1987 storm and areas of non-intervention management. Areas of coppice and old wood pasture, with scattered ancient pollards and associated ground flora. A sense of seclusion and isolation within this ancient landscape is there to be enjoyed. Gumber Bothy provides basic accommodation (self-catering) for walkers, cyclists and horse riders, 500m. off the South Downs Way. Tel. (01243) 814484.

Open: Free access, dawn to dusk, all year. Extensive network of rights of way (footpaths and bridleways), and woodland rides.

16. ST. LEONARD'S FOREST
HORSHAM
Tel: (01420) 23666
TQ207298

(Forest Enterprise)   242 ha. (598 acres)

From Horsham, take the A281 to Mannings Heath.   Take the minor road running from Mannings Heath. After just over ½ mile, turn L at the T-junction and the car park is on the R, some 400 yards distant.

St. Leonards was once part of the great forest of Anderida which stretched 100 miles east to west between the north and south Downs.   Today it covers only 12 square miles but is part of the High Weald Area of Outstanding Natural Beauty.   The woodlands are a varied mixture, ranging from ancient woodland relics along the stream-sides, through patches of old oak woodland, to plantations of Scots and Corsican pine. The forest is criss-crossed by a myriad of small paths and rides.   Some damage from the great storm of 1987 is still visible, but younger trees are beginning to colonise the open spaces created.

Open: Free access at all times. Waymarked walk. Horse riding by permit.

---

17. STANSTED FOREST
ROWLANDS CASTLE
Tel: (01705) 412265
SU753105

(Stansted Park Foundation)
400 ha. (988 acres)

Centre of Excellence

From Rowlands Castle, take Woodberry Lane SE for 1½ miles; then L and L again. Forest car park is 1 mile N on L.

A large area of diverse, mainly broadleaved, woodland incorporating wildlife habitats and landscape features. Many large, ancient, environmentally important trees and over 200 species of flowering plants recorded. The main avenue over 1½ miles long is one of the longest beech avenues in England.

Open: Free access at all times. Public and permissive rights of way (please keep to tracks and rides). Some areas are private.

---

18. WOOLBEDING WOOD
WOOLBEDING
Tel: (01730) 816638
SU868232

(National Trust)   9 ha. (22 acres)

Woolbeding Wood is just NW of Midhurst. Access via footpath 1128, at SU868232 (adjacent to Bramblings Farm), or from a NT permitted path which runs through the river fields (which often have stock in), at the foot of the wood (SU871222). A pair of woodland rides join these two paths together to make a very pleasant circular walk.

The wood is situated on a steep west facing slope above the river Rother. It is undoubtedly an ancient woodland site and parts of it contain important semi-natural stand types like the old beeches at the northern end. National Trust management is for nature conservation and quiet enjoyment.

Open: Free access dawn to dusk, all year. One public footpath. Several permitted paths/rides.

Woods for learning

These woods are particularly well organised for school and group visits. Most of them offer information leaflets, guided walks, self-guided trails, and educational materials. Telephone the contact number of the wood to arrange your visit, including coach parking arrangements if necessary.

As well as the woods listed below, you will see in the gazeteer that many others have self-guided trails or offer guided walks, and could make an interesting destination for an organised outing. More such facilities are being added every year, so it is worth 'phoning to check the current position.

East Sussex:

Abbots Wood
Coney Burrow
Friston Forest
Powdermill Wood
Wilderness Wood

Hampshire/Isle of Wight:

Alice Holt Woodland Park
Firestone Copse
Morgaston Wood
New Forest
Pamber Forest
Parkhurst Forest
Queen Elizabeth Country Park
Town and Walters Copse

Kent:

Bedgebury Pinetum
Blean Woods Nature Reserve
Bushy, Batfold and Kilnhouse Woods
Shorne Wood Country Park
Trosley Country Park

Surrey:

Box Hill
Hindhead Woods
Leith Hill
Nower Wood
Winterfold Forest
Wiltey Common

West Sussex:

Borde Hill Gardens
Harting Down Local Nature Reserve
Leechpool and Owlbeech Woods
Slindon Woods

The Forest Education Initiative

The Forest Education Initiative (FEI) brings together people who grow and use timber with those who work in education. It aims to increase young people's understanding of the local and global importance of trees, woodlands, the forestry industry and the timber trade, and the links between them.

FEI cluster groups are being developed throughout Britain. These local clusters bring together teachers, foresters, timber processors and manufacturers who provide local information and resources for schools. They may hold teachers' workshops and enable schools to organise first-hand learning experiences for pupils in local woods, paper and saw mills and factories.

Information on the **Kent and Medway cluster** can be obtained from Rosemary Clark (Tel. 01622 884422). If you are interested in being part of a new cluster in your area, contact the co-ordinator, Margaret Hardy, Great Eastern House, Tenison Road, Cambridge CB1 2DU (Tel. 01223 314546).

The FEI teaching packs help young people to make connections between sustainable, multi-purpose woodlands and how wood is used. Three new illustrated books, written by teachers, suggest activities to explore forestry, timber processing and products; trade and international development; recreation, conservation and economic issues in today's woods and forests, both locally and globally.

"Only Made of Wood"

Only Made of Wood is an exciting new resource for infants. Designed for 5 to 7 year olds, it consists of a beautifully illustrated storybook and a photocopiable teacher's book packed with ideas for indoor and outdoor activities. The full colour storybook uses simple language to tell the story of a wooden rocking horse that comes to life and takes two children on a magical woodland adventure. The activities focus on trees, wood and paper and can be used to develop skills and knowledge in English and other curriculum areas. A table of curriculum references is provided. The pack costs £11.90, plus £1.25 p&p, and can be obtained from Biblios PDS Ltd., Star Road, Partridge Green, West Sussex RH13 8LD. Cheques should be made payable to Biblios PDS.

The Wonder of Wood

The Wonder of Wood is an activity based resource for 7 to 11 year olds. Silva the owl encourages children to look at trees and the uses of wood locally and in other parts of the world. Photocopiable worksheets are amplified by teachers' notes and suggestions for further activities. Guidelines link the activities to the National Curriculum Key Stage 2 and the Scottish 5-14 Curriculum. The pack costs £9.50 including p&p and can be obtained from the FEI Co-ordinator, Great Eastern House, Tenison Road Cambridge CB1 2DU. Cheques should be made payable to Forest Education Initiative.

Investigating Trees and Timber

Investigating Trees and Timber and its three colour posters help secondary pupils to explore the role of timber in our lives. I investigates trees, forests and timber in the UK and their importance for communitie in other parts of the world, using France an Ghana as examples. Aimed at 14 to 16 yea olds, it has links with Geography, Science Technology, Business Studies and PSE. Th pack costs £11.50 including p&p and can b ordered from the FEI Co-ordinator, Grea Eastern House, Tenison Road, Cambridg CB1 2DU. Cheques should be mad payable to Forest Education Initiative.

Where to find out more

Arboricultural Association

Ampfield House, Ampfield, Romsey, Hants. SO51 9PA.
Tel: (01794) 68717

Aims to raise the standards of tree care in Britain. Journal, newsletter, directories of registered arboricultural consultants and contractors.

British Trust for Conservation Volunteers

36 St. Mary's Street, Wallingford, Oxon. OX10 0EU.
Tel: (01491) 839766
Fax: (01491) 839646

A national body with a large network of local field officers throughout the country. They provide training, advice and support for volunteers, local groups and schools.

Common Ground

Seven Dials Warehouse, 44 Earlham Street, London WC2H 9LA.
Tel: 0171 379 3109
Fax: 0171 836 5741

Aims to give inspiration, information and ideas to help people explore their local surroundings. Works through projects such as "Trees, Woods and the Green Man", Apple Days, Tree Dressing Days, Community Orchards. Send sae for publication list.

Council for Environmental Education

University of Reading, London Road, Reading RG1 5AQ
Tel: (0118) 9756061
Fax: (0118) 9756264

CEE provides a national focus in England encouraging and promoting an environmental approach to education. Publications include regular newsheets and information sheets including one on Trees, Woods, Forests and Rainforests).

Country Landowners' Association

16 Belgrave Square, London SW1X 8PQ
Tel: 0171 235 0511   Fax: 0171 235 4696

The CLA supports co-operation to provide more access for everyone wanting to use and enjoy the countryside. Through its Access 2000 initiative, the CLA has promised to deliver a net gain in the quality, diversity and quantity of access in the countryside through voluntary agreements. By encouraging a positive approach, the CLA has helped the Forestry Trust in securing the co-operation of private woodland owners to provide public access and to allow their woods to appear in Exploring Woodlands in the South East.

Countryside Commission

John Dower House, Crescent Place, Cheltenham, GL50 3RA.
Tel: (01242) 521381
Fax: (01242) 584270

The official body for countryside conservation and recreation in England. An advisory and promotional organisation which works in partnership with others. Has spearheaded the development of the National Forest and 12 Community Forests.

Council for the Protection of Rural England

Warwick House, 25 Buckingham Palace Road, London SW1W 0PP.
Tel: 0171 976 6433
Fax: 0171 976 6373

Campaigns for the protection and enhancement of the countryside. Produces a general leaflet on the value of trees, and a Campaigners' Guide to Trees and Woods which details the opportunities for people to influence decisions affecting the planting, felling and management of trees and woods.

English Nature

Northminster House, Peterborough PE1 1UA.
Tel: (01733) 455000

The government's official adviser on nature conservation in England. Currently running an initiative on "Veteran Trees" to highlight their value culturally, in the landscape and for wildlife. Useful leaflets include "English woodland and nature conservation", "Guide to the care of ancient trees", a poster/leaflet "Veteran trees", and "Guidelines for identifying ancient woodland".

Forest Education Initiative

Great Eastern House, Tenison Road, Cambridge CB1 2DU.
Tel: (01223) 314546
Fax: (01223) 460699

Publishes teaching packs about trees, woodlands and forestry. Developing a network of local forest education groups who can organise visits and activities for schools.

Forestry Commission
(Enterprise and Authority)

231 Corstorphine Road, Edinburgh EH12 7AT
Tel: 0131 334 0303
Fax: 0131 334 4473

Government department responsible for promoting sustainable, multipurpose forestry in Great Britain. Provides information, advice and extensive list of publications from the Information Division in Edinburgh. Free teachers' pack includes list of regional centres which provide visitor services and publications on local forests and woodlands.

The Forestry Trust for Conservation and Education

The Old Estate Office, Englefield Road, Theale, Reading, RG7 5DZ.
Tel: (0118) 9323523
Fax: (0118) 9304033

Promotes understanding of the many roles of forestry through publications and an enquiry service. Publications include identification guides, posters and "Tree and Timber" data sheets. The Trust is organising a number of Forest Friends Partnerships (FFP'S) in England and Wales to provide educational visits to selected woods.

Forests Forever!

4th Floor, Clareville House, 26/27 Oxenden Street, London SW1Y 4EL.
Tel: 0171 839 189
Fax: 0171 930 0094

The Forests Forever Campaign is working to ensure the future of forests around the world for centuries to come. It is an inititaive of the Timber Trades Federation, supported by timber related companies of all types. The two main objectives of the campaign are to encourage forested countries to operate "best practice" forest management, including replanting, and to encourage informed debate about our need for wood and wood products and their sources.

Institute of Chartered Foresters

7a St Colme Street, Edinburgh EH3 6AA
Tel: 0131 225 2705

Aims to maintain and improve the standards of practice of forestry, and encourage its study. Journal, newsletter, meetings, directory of members in consultany practice.

International Tree Foundation

Sandy Lane, Crawley Down, West Sussex RH10 4HS.
Tel: (01342) 712536
Fax: (01342) 718282

Promotes an appreciation of trees and encourages their planting, care and protection. Produces quarterly newsletters, an annual yearbook and organised activities and events at county branch level.

National Small Woods Association

Hall Farm House, Preston Capes, Northants.
Tel: (01327) 361225

Promotes management, conservation and rehabilitation of small and neglected woods. Newsletter, training courses and seminars.

National Trust

36 Qeen Anne's Gate, London SW8 2XX
Tel: 0171 222 9251
Fax: 0171 222 5097

Protects beautiful and precious countryside and buildings.

Ramblers' Association

1-5 Wandsworth Road, London SW8 2XX.
Tel: 0171 582 6878

Promotes the interests of walkers, and

countryside access.

The Royal Forestry Society

102 High Street, Tring, Herts. HP23 4AF.
Tel: (01442) 822028
Fax: (01442) 890395
Website: http://www.rfs.org.uk/

The RFS promotes understanding of trees and forestry in England, Wales and Northern Ireland and the conservation and expansion of tree resources through good forestry management which takes into account their wildlife, landscape, recreational and socio-economic value.

The RFS is the largest forestry association in Britain, with more than 4,500 members. The membership is broadly based, bringing together all those interested in trees - woodland owners, foresters, arboriculturalists, land managers, conservationists and the general public.

The RFS provides opportunities for everyone to extend their knowledge and appreciation of trees and woodlands. Over 100 local and national field meetings are held each year where members can exchange views and see and discuss examples of practical woodland management.

Members receive the Quarterly Journal of Forestry, and new members are especially welcomed.

Royal Society for the Protection of Birds

The Lodge, Sandy, Beds. SG19 2DL.
Tel: (01767) 680551

Takes action to protect wild birds and their environment.

Timber Growers Association

Dublin Street Lane South, Edinburgh EH1 PX.
Tel: 0131 557 0944

Represents woodland owners and forestry buisnesses. Journal, newsletter, publications, helplines.

The Tree Council

1 Catherine Place, London SW1E 6DY.
Tel: 0171 828 9928
Fax: 0171 828 9060

Co-ordinating body for many organisations concerned with trees. Promotes the protection of trees and woodlands and encourages new planting. Organises Esso National Tree Week, Esso Walk in the Woods and a national Tree Warden Scheme. Publishes "Tree News" and various books and leaflets.

Trees of Time and Place

Mailpoint 512, 96 Victoria Street, London SW1E 5JW.
Tel: Hotline (0345) 078139
(local call rate)

Trees of Time and Place is a campaign to help millions of people to grow a personal tree from seed and plant it locally to mark the new millennium. England is one of the least wooded countries in Europe and Trees of Time and Place has been set up to help everyone contribute towards increasing our woodlands. A wide range of organisations are working together in support of the campaign to help people visit woodlands, and to help them grow and plant their personal tree seedlings. With your support the campaign can make sure that future generations can enjoy the benefit from our woodlands. Find out how you can get involved by calling 0345 078139, or visit our website at www.totap.org.uk.

The Wildlife Trusts

The Green, Witham Park, Waterside South, Lincoln LN5 2JR.
Tel: (01522) 544400
Fax: (01522) 511616

A partnership of 47 county wildlife trusts and urban wildlife groups. Wildlife Watch is the junior section of the Trust and has a network of local groups.

The Woodland Trust

Autumn Park, Dysart Road, Grantham, Lincs. NG31 6LL.
Tel: (01476) 581111
Fax: (01476) 590808

Promotes the conservation and protection of mainly native trees and woods. Has an active programme of acquiring woodlands of all sizes, especially those under threat. Also plants trees to create new woods. Produces a range of information materials.

Read all about it

Trees and their identification

The Mitchell Beazley Pocket Guide to Trees. By Keith Rushforth. Mitchell Beazley Publishers Ltd., 1980. ISBN 0 85533 267 0   Inexpensive, reliable and well illustrated, covers a large number of trees. Easy to use.

A Field Guide to the Trees of Britain and Northern Europe. By Alan Mitchell. Collins 1974 and several subsequent editions. ISBN 0 00 212035 6 The standard text book on tree identification and correct names but not easy for the amateur to use.

The Trees of Britain and Northern Europe. By Alan Mitchell. Collins 1982. ISBN 0 00 219035 4 (paper back) 0 00 219037 0 (hardback).   Descriptions of the trees rather than identification details and not well illustrated.

Field Guide to the Trees of Britain and Europe. By David Sutton. Kingfisher Books 1990. ISBN 0-86272-523-2   An inexpensive and well illustrated and comprehensive book, easy to use.

Trees in Britain, Europe and North America. By Roger Phillips. Pan Books Ltd. ISBN 0 330 25480 4.   High quality photographs with brief identification notes.

The Guinness Book of Trees By Esmond & Jeanette Harris. Guideway Publishing Ltd. 1981. ISBN 0-85112-303-1   Simple text on the origin of trees and their place in Britain and how they grow. Includes identification notes and illustrations of the 50 most common trees

found in Britain, including introduced commercial species. Out of print but available in most libraries.

Alan Mitchell's Trees of Britain. By Alan Mitchell. HarperCollins 1996. ISBN 0 00 219213 6   A very personal and readable account of how the many trees, both native and introduced, grow in Britain and where the best specimens can be found.

Hugh Johnson's Encyclopaedia of Trees. By Hugh Johnson. Mitchell Beazley 1984. ISBN 0 85533 546 7.   The second edition of the original International Book of Trees. A large, well illustrated 'coffee table' book with a wealth of information on trees throughout the world.

Pocket Guide to the Wildlife of Britain and Europe. By Jeanette Harris. Kingfisher Books 1983 & 1985. ISBN 0 86272 048 6.   First published in 1981 as the Kingfisher Nature Handbook. Very comprehensive and well illustrated with simple identification notes on trees and all other forms of wildlife.

For children

Spotter's Guide to Trees. By Esmond Harris. Usborne Publishing Ltd., 1978. ISBN 0 86020 106 6 (paper back) 0 86020 107 4 (hard back).   Forms part of the excellent Usborne series for children. Illustrations with simple identification notes on 48 common trees.

Spotter's Handbook – British Flowers, Trees and Birds. Usborne Publishing Ltd., 1978. ISBN 0 86020 159 7   Includes the tree material from the Spotter's Guide to Trees and quizzes and puzzles for children.

Spotter's Guide to Woodland Life. By Sue Jacquemier. Usborne Publishing Ltd., 1979. ISBN 0 86020 286 0 (paper back) 0 86020 287 9 (hard back). An identification guide for children to to all the wildlife found in woodlands.

The Nature Trail Book of Trees and Leaves. By Ingrid Selberg. Usborne Publishing Ltd., 1977. ISBN 0 86020 099 X (paper back) 0 86020 100 7 (hard back). A practical guide for children with colour illustrations and things do with trees; includes simple identification notes. Used widely by schools.

Usborne First Nature - Trees. By Ruth Thomson. Usborne Publishing Ltd., 1980. ISBN 0 86020 473 1. A simple text and illustrations suitable for small children on trees and how they grow; includes activities and puzzles.

Woodland management and history

Wildlife Conservation in Managed Woodlands and Forests. By Esmond Harris & Jeanette Harris. Research Studies Press Ltd., 1997. ISBN 0 86380 206 0. A comprehensive textbook on the integration of wildlife conservation within productive woods; includes detailed notes all the wildlife species found in woodlands and forests.

The International Book of the Forest. By a wide variety of international authors. Mitchell Beazley 1981. ISBN 0 85533 345 . A detailed account of forests throughout the world.

Traditional Woodland Crafts. By Raymond Tabor. Batsford 1994. ISBN 0 134 7138 7. Describes traditional coppice management and crafts associated with it as they are being increasingly practiced again today.

Trees and Woodland in the British Landscape. By Oliver Rackham. J.M.Dent & Sons Ltd 1976. ISBN 0 460 02223 7. A personal view of how woods have been managed in the past and have arrived at their present condition.

Index